EVERY SHOT
MUST HAVE
A PURPOSE

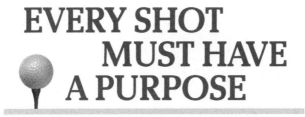

EVERY SHOT MUST HAVE A PURPOSE

Pia Nilsson and Lynn Marriott
with Ron Sirak

GOTHAM BOOKS

GOTHAM BOOKS
Published by Penguin Group (USA) Inc.
375 Hudson Street, New York, New York 10014, U.S.A.

Penguin Group (Canada), 90 Eglinton Avenue East, Suite 700, Toronto, Ontario
M4P 2Y3, Canada (a division of Pearson Penguin Canada Inc.); Penguin Books Ltd, 80
Strand, London WC2R 0RL, England; Penguin Ireland, 25 St Stephen's Green, Dublin 2,
Ireland (a division of Penguin Books Ltd); Penguin Group (Australia), 250 Camberwell
Road, Camberwell, Victoria 3124, Australia (a division of Pearson Australia Group Pty Ltd);
Penguin Books India Pvt Ltd, 11 Community Centre, Panchsheel Park, New Delhi–
110 017, India; Penguin Group (NZ), cnr Airborne and Rosedale Roads, Albany, Auckland
1310, New Zealand (a division of Pearson New Zealand Ltd); Penguin Books
(South Africa) (Pty) Ltd, 24 Sturdee Avenue, Rosebank, Johannesburg 2196, South Africa

Penguin Books Ltd, Registered Offices: 80 Strand, London WC2R 0RL, England

Published by Gotham Books, a member of Penguin Group (USA) Inc.

First printing, September 2005
10 9 8 7 6

Gotham Books and the skyscraper logo are trademarks of Penguin Group (USA) Inc.

LIBRARY OF CONGRESS CATALOGING-IN-PUBLICATION DATA
has been applied for.

ISBN 1-592-40157-0

GOLF54®, VISION54®, HEARTGOLF®, GOOD-BETTER-HOW?™ are registered
trademarks of Pia Nilsson and Lynn Marriott.

Permission to use copyrighted information on the HeartMath® technique and Quick Co-
herence® was granted by Howard Martin and Gabriella Boehmer at HeartMath. Any use
of this material in a derivative work is not permitted without written permission from
HeartMath® System; 14700 West Park Avenue; Boulder Creek, CA 95006.

Illustration by Laura Hartman Maestro

Printed in the United States of America
Set in Bembo with OPTI Carvery
Designed by Daniel Lagin

Contents

Acknowledgments   xi

Foreword: **By Annika Sorenstam**   xv

INTRODUCTION
Imagine the Impossible; Then Figure Out How
to Make It Happen
By Ron Sirak   xix

CHAPTER I
Forget What You Know, Learn What You Know   1

CHAPTER II
Change Your Brain to Change Your Game   13

CHAPTER III
Think Inside the Box   22

CHAPTER IV
Think Small, Play Big   33

CHAPTER V
The Most Important Shot in Golf Is This One   45

CHAPTER VI
You Are More Consistent Than You Think   53

CHAPTER VII
Anger Makes Us Stupid   61

CHAPTER VIII
Don't Play the Blame Game   72

CHAPTER IX
Let the Target Be Your Guide   81

CHAPTER X
Make Practice Real: Practice with a Purpose   88

CHAPTER XI
Play with a Purpose: Don't Try a Shot
You Can't Handle   99

CHAPTER XII
Send Your Mind on Vacation   107

CHAPTER XIII
See the Putt from Behind the Ball,
Then Trust What You See   115

CHAPTER XIV
Golf Is About Getting the Ball in the Hole   123

CHAPTER XV
HEARTGOLF: It All Adds Up to Better Golf   128

CHAPTER XVI
Make Pressure Your Friend   140

CHAPTER XVII
It's All About the Person First   151

CHAPTER XVIII
Have a Swing That Suits You   162

CHAPTER XIX
The 54-Shot Challenge   170

CHAPTER XX
The 30-Ball Practice Drill   180

CHAPTER XXI
Good–Better–How?   186

CHAPTER XXII
VISION54: Make It the Way You See the Game   193

Recommended Reading   199

GOLF54 Programs   200

Acknowledgments

We want to thank the game of golf. Golf has inspired us immeasurably. It has focused our hearts to look deeper and wider and to act with congruency to our purpose. We appreciate the game, in all its dimensions, as it has engaged our courage to make decisions and commit to them and to continue to learn.

Thank you, Annika, for striving for excellence and motivating and testing us to become better coaches.

Thanks to all the players we have had the privilege to coach. They have always been our greatest source of motivation, feedback, and learning.

Thank you to the many teachers and mentors we have been blessed with in our lives. To name a few who have profoundly influenced us: Chuck Hogan, Ken Blanchard, Annette Thompson, Michael Murphy, Manuel de la Torre, Pam Barnett, Kjell Enhager, Jorunn Sjobakken, and Truls Fleiner.

Thank you to our friend Susan Reed for taking us by the hand to find a book agent and always being supportive. Mark

Reiter, thank you for finding us a great publisher. Bill Shinker and Erin Moore, the two of you have been fun and easy to work with. We appreciate that you have really cared about our book and its purpose.

Ron, thank you for saying yes to working with us. The three of us have been a true team without any egos involved and a whole lot of heart! Thanks for helping us put our thoughts on paper in a way we never could have imagined. We have met many golf writers who only see the game from a limited perspective; Ron Sirak has a love for the game and enthusiastically embraced the bigger picture. We often say, "How did we get so blessed to work with Ron?"

Finally, thanks and "tack" to our parents. They have genuinely supported us in our efforts to find our way and be who we are. With unconditional love they steadfastly encouraged us to find our purpose and to stay on purpose. They allowed us to take both risks and responsibility and to believe that anything is possible.

Lynn Marriott and Pia Nilsson
Phoenix, Arizona, and Torekov, Sweden
2005

This book, or at least my involvement in this book, would not have happened if Annika Sorenstam had not decided to play in the 2003 Bank of America Colonial. It was through my efforts to understand what motivated Annika to take her game to the men's tour that I came to know Lynn Marriott and Pia

Nilsson. That first round of competition by Annika at Colonial was the single most exciting day I have spent at a sporting event in more than thirty years as a journalist. I thank Annika for that thrill, and I thank her for creating a situation that exposed me to VISION54 and, ultimately, GOLF54. I thank her also for her generous kindness as a friend and patient understanding as a professional.

I have been fortunate in my career to work with some extremely talented editors, starting with Lamar Hoover at the Lancaster (Pennsylvania) Independent Press through Bill Ahern, Brian Friedman, and Rich Herzfelder at The Associated Press. At *Golf World,* I work with three of the best: Tim Murphy, Bill Fields, and Geoff Russell, an editor-in-chief who has made a great magazine even better. I owe double thanks to Jerry Tarde, the chairman and editorial director of The Golf Digest Companies, first for bringing me on board, and secondly for refusing to let me leave. Thanks also go to Advance Magazines Publishers, Inc., for its tireless commitment to quality journalism.

My agent, Mark Reiter of PFD, believed in this project from the very beginning and was the glue that brought all of us together. The reaction of Bill Shinker of Gotham Books to the first draft of the manuscript was one of the nicest compliments I have received as a journalist. His enthusiasm for golf, and for GOLF54, was a constant source of inspiration. The work of Erin Moore at Gotham Books puts her high on my list of quality editors. I can't thank her enough for shepherding the book through its most difficult phase: actually bringing it into being.

My thanks go to my daughter, Rachel Sirak, for constantly reminding me that I have a cool job. Thanks also to Sarah Goldstein, who has the true soul of an artist, and Hannah Goldstein, who might be the smartest gymnast ever to stick a dismount. I thank Doug Ferguson of the AP for being a sounding board for what is real, and Jim Litke of the AP for being a sounding board for what is surreal. Thanks to Chris Penberthy for making me go to London, a place where I surely lived in another life.

Finally, thank you to Lynn Marriott and Pia Nilsson for allowing me into their lives. They are not only uncommon educators in the game of golf, they are uncommon educators in the game of life. I have always felt that Dr. Solomon Wank at Franklin & Marshall College was the best teacher I have ever had. Dr. Wank now shares that position with Lynn and Pia. They've made me not only a better golfer, but also a better writer and a better person. My thanks to them for trusting me with this project. It's more than golf instruction, it's a way of life. And I am better for having learned it.

Ron Sirak
Bridgeport, Connecticut
2005

Foreword

Annika Sorenstam

The first time I heard the notion of VISION54 was in 1989. I was eighteen years old and playing for Pia Nilsson on the Swedish National Team. Being the numbers cruncher that I am, the idea of following a systematic road map to perfection immediately captured my attention. The idea that I could birdie every hole on any golf course in the same round (because, at one time or another, I had birdied every hole on my home course) truly motivated me. As an extremely competitive person, I loved the idea of breaking down barriers and seeking new challenges. Why should par be the standard we hold ourselves to? Why not birdie? Why should two putts per green be considered routine? Why not one? VISION54 knocked down the walls around my imagination and set it free.

But the idea of VISION54 that was born in Sweden was just the beginning. In that concept is the ideal of excellence that we strive toward. It is the goal. What Pia and Lynn Marriott did through years of work and research in the United States was develop a toolbox—a method—to get the player on the path to excellence. It is that system, GOLF54, that you will learn about in this book. The first step is VISION54—the belief that you can achieve your full potential. The subsequent steps are GOLF54—the tools you need to approach that potential. Pia and Lynn have developed a method that can put players of any level on a path to better performance.

I won the U.S. Women's Open in 1995, when I was just twenty-four years old, and again in 1996. In my first six years on the LPGA I won eighteen tournaments and was one of the best players in the world. But I wanted to be the absolute best. What I did after the 1999 season is what this book is all about. I realized that achieving my goal of being Number 1 was not a matter of improving my swing; it was about me improving as a total player—and as a person. It was about me trying to figure out what this game is all about and develop a strategy to play it at its highest level.

I decided that to get to the next level I had to be the best at everything. I dissected all aspects of the game in order to understand what I had to do to try to improve. I wanted my swing to be able to repeat reliably under the most intense pressure, and worked with my coach, Henri Reis, to make it even better. I wanted to be the fittest player on tour so I hired my trainer, Kai Fusser, and started a workout program that, so far, has added thirty yards to my tee shots. I wanted to be the strongest mentally and talked more with Pia and Lynn about achieving the discipline necessary for that goal. I wanted to be the best putter and, that winter, I spent six weeks totally dedicated to putting. I wanted to be the best chipper and the best at distance control, so I worked on many of the drills you will learn about in this book.

What I learned from the 1999 season was this: Improvement as a player is not just about sharpening your skills. It is also about getting better as a person. That is part of the magic of GOLF54. It teaches you not just about golf but also about yourself. Pia and Lynn are not just about the golf swing. They know so much more about the game and so much more about people. Their approach to instruction is very individual. When they talk to me about how I should handle a certain situation, they are talking to ME. Instead of trying to fit me into a mold, they help me understand my shape and what works best for me. They look at each individual as a unique person. And they understand that golf is about more than just the grip, the stance, and the swing: It is about the person.

When I played against the men at Colonial, everything I had in my bag helped me. I had the confidence I had gained from all my success on the LPGA Tour. I had the emotional resolve I had accumulated by winning major championships. Colonial was a moment of enormous pressure. The whole world was watching me. We all have experiences and we all have memories and they will be there forever. What we need to do is learn how to use those positive memories and dissociate from the negative ones. I have never been more nervous hitting a golf shot than that first drive at Colonial. But I was able to focus my mind on only one thing—hitting that golf shot. And I could not have hit it better. What Pia and Lynn teach in this book is how to achieve that focus.

This book will make you a better golfer, but what it is truly about is making you better as a person. For all of us—even those of us who play the game on the professional level—it is essential to remember that we are not golfers who happen to be people but rather we are people who happen to play golf. It doesn't matter if you are trying to break 100 or if you are trying to break 60—we can all get better at whatever level we are on. You need to look at yourself and see what you have to do better. It is all about being honest with yourself, identifying your weaknesses, and dealing with them. There are always excuses that are easy to hide behind, but you have to learn to focus on the things that you can control and never let excuses get in the way of performance and improvement. This book will show you the way.

When you get right down to it, golf is about one thing—putting the ball in the hole. And when you break it down even further, all you can do is hit the ball, go find it, and hit it again. The key to how successfully you hit the ball is to make clear decisions and to hit each shot with total commitment to those decisions. VISION54 created a sparkling ideal in my mind, and GOLF54 provided the pathway toward it. This book will help you find your personal pathway to improvement. It will teach you how to make clear, committed decisions. This book will teach you how to play better golf. And, most importantly, this book will show you how to make golf more fun than you ever imagined. Here's to hoping you find your VISION54 just as I have! And here's to knowing you'll have fun pursuing it.

INTRODUCTION

Imagine the Impossible; Then Figure Out How to Make It Happen

Ron Sirak

"The secret of success is constancy to purpose."
—BENJAMIN DISRAELI, NINETEENTH-CENTURY
ENGLISH PRIME MINISTER

What you are about to read is a golf book unlike any other. Through years of teaching players of all different skill levels—from beginners to top professionals—Pia Nilsson and Lynn Marriott have refined an approach to instruction that is not bogged down in arm angles, spine positions, and swing thoughts so complex they would make the average golfer's brain freeze with confused indecision. Rather, VISION54, the revolutionary approach to the game that Pia developed in Sweden twenty years ago and that she refined with Lynn as GOLF54, teaches that peak performance on the golf course is achieved by simplifying the game, not by burdening the pupil with overly technical instruction. As Pia and Lynn say, "It's all about the person first."

What you will find in these pages is a life philosophy, not merely a golf instruction book. It is the most radical departure from traditional golf instruction yet to come along. VISION54 teaches us to expand our concept of limits. GOLF54 provides the tools that make it possible for us to achieve our vision. The intuitive intelligence of Pia and Lynn's approach reduces the game to such a basic and accessible level that you will frequently find yourself, as I did, shaking your head and saying, "Of course," when they point out an obvious aspect of the game that has been obscured by what they call the Pez Dispenser School of Instruction—"Bend your knees, thirty bucks please." GOLF54 takes us back to the reason we started to play golf in the first place: It's fun. It is in the rediscovery of that joy that Pia and Lynn teach us how to find the keys to better play.

One of the disturbing trends the golf industry has to confront is the fact that in the United States as many people quit the game each year as take it up. While cost and the time required to play a round of golf are significant reasons for this trend, many are also driven away because the game becomes more of a struggle than an enjoyable experience. When a troubled golfer tries to get help, he or she will most likely be given a series of instructions that would require a much more talented athlete and a serious amount of time to master. Completely rebuilding a swing is not only impractical for most players, it is also unnecessary. You have hit good shots with the swing you have. You have hit perfect shots with the swing you have. This book will teach you how to make those shots happen more often. You don't need a new swing; you need a more defined sense of purpose.

I had known about Pia for many years as a player, a coach, and a European Solheim Cup captain, and had long been fascinated by her novel approach to instruction. I knew of her astonishing success with Annika Sorenstam and I was aware of the rebellion against her by some of the tradition-bound players when she tried to bring her innovative approach to the 1998 Solheim Cup team. But I did not really get to know Pia and Lynn until 2003, when Sorenstam decided she would play in a men's event on the PGA Tour. I interviewed Pia soon after Annika announced her intentions and revisited the conversation several times in the months leading up to the Bank of America Colonial. After listening carefully to Annika's words, a light went on in my head. "Of course," I said to myself. "It's so obvious." Words you will say time and again as you read this book.

I called Pia and said, "It doesn't matter what Annika shoots at Colonial, right? And it doesn't even matter if she makes the cut, right? All that matters for Annika to consider the experience a success is if she feels she has handled the enormity of the moment well." Pia, who punctuates life with an exclamation point, laughed and said, "You got it!" I know some teachers who would have then added, "What took you so long?" But that is not the way of Pia and Lynn. They lead you to knowledge. Understanding is up to you. Commitment is up to you. Sorenstam did not make the cut at Colonial, but her opening round of 71 was a ball-striking performance of such perfection that women's golf gained new respect instantly and more than just fans of the LPGA finally appreciated Annika's skills. GOLF54 was a key component in how well Annika handled the pressure of that day.

It was at Colonial that I had my first extensive conversation with Lynn Marriott, who has been a Class A teaching professional since 1983. Lynn graduated cum laude with a degree in marketing and management from Penn State University, but she could just as easily hang out her shingle as a psychologist. Her numerous courses and seminars have as much to do with communication, leadership, mental training, and the psychology of how to coach as they do with golf. It was Lynn who made THINK BOX/PLAY BOX, which is so essential to GOLF54 teaching, come to life, and made it a real experience. If Pia punctuates life with an exclamation point, Lynn approaches the process with a question mark. Like any good therapist, she provides answers by asking shrewd questions. Lynn has always had a vision of a whole-game approach. It was clear to her as a young teacher that the golf swing does not equal golf.

In April of 2004, I went to Pia and Lynn's school at the Legacy Golf Resort in Phoenix. When I left for three days of instruction, friends who had been to other golf schools told me how much my hands would hurt and my muscles would ache after days of beating balls. Clearly, they had never been students of Pia and Lynn. The biggest breakthroughs were made when the ten of us in the class were sitting in a circle, laughing and collectively grasping one of their concepts. As much was accomplished in discussions over dinner or lunch as was accomplished on the range. When we hit balls or when we went out onto the course it was with the drills and exercises you will learn in these pages. Instead of complex theory, we learned the focus that allows the good shots within us to come out more often. We practiced with a purpose, and we played with a purpose.

I wish I had met Pia and Lynn years ago. Not just because it would have helped my game—which it has—but also because it would have made me a better golf writer. Now, since I understand their method better, I understand Annika Sorenstam better. I look at her with new eyes and appreciate that everything she does at a tournament—from where she stays and whom she stays with to where she eats and when she practices and how she practices—has a purpose. I watch her routine on the golf course and I smile inwardly when she steps into the THINK BOX and then moves with total commitment across the DECISION LINE into the PLAY BOX.

I watch other players, and when they struggle I can spot the physical and mental errors Pia and Lynn have taught me to be aware of in my own game. I also wish I had met Pia and Lynn earlier because, in addition to improving me as a player and as a writer—I now employ many of the philosophies in this book in the way I approach work—they have also improved me as a person. They are two very special people whose approach to teaching is rooted not just in a love of the game but also in an appreciation of and respect for the individual.

Their approach—GOLF54—will teach you how to develop

routines you can trust and it will teach you how to transfer those routines from the practice range to the golf course. It will teach you how to embrace your ability and how to discover, in that embrace, the secrets of moving closer to achieving your ultimate potential. There is good golf within you. Pia and Lynn will help you bring it out more often.

CHAPTER I

Forget What You Know, Learn What You Know

"Learning is experience. Everything else is just information."

—ALBERT EINSTEIN, TWENTIETH-CENTURY SCIENTIST

SWING KEY: Empty your head so wisdom can flow in.

All golf instruction books promise to lower your score. We promise to make you a better player. You decide what that will do for your handicap. What we offer is not a quick fix providing temporary results but rather a new perspective that will allow you to maximize your abilities and approach your peak performance more often—and more reliably under pressure—no matter what your skill level. We will show you how to become much more than a mere student of the swing. If you are a beginner, you will learn how to play better sooner on the golf course. If you have been playing for a while, you will learn how to score lower. No matter what your skill level, you will learn how to enjoy the game more. You will learn how to make golf a game you love, not one you fear.

How are we going to make you a better player? Well, it is absurd to think that we can change your swing with a book. For one thing, we've never seen your swing. How can we change it? While there are certain mechanical fundamentals essential to playing the game—grip, stance, posture, etc.—we believe there is more than one right way to swing a golf club. And we believe that golf is far more than merely the physical act of swinging a club. Your fundamental problems are probably not with the way you swing but rather with the way you approach the game.

How many times have you taken a swing tip to the golf course and found that it was a magic elixir for a few rounds, only to wear off when you needed it most? How many times have you hit the ball great on the range only to lose it when the round starts? That's because traditional instruction separates the swing from the person, and it separates practice from real golf. We integrate the two. GOLF54 is not about teaching; it is about learning. Most approaches to instruction focus on the teacher's knowledge; we focus on the student's potential. **A lesson well learned becomes your teacher for life.** Everyone who swings a golf club has hit a good shot at one time or another. We will show you how to open the door that will allow those good shots to come out more often.

What we offer is a radical departure from traditional golf instruction. The current culture of instruction leads you to believe that the technical is the only piece of the puzzle that matters. This kind of teaching reduces the gloriously fluid, decidedly sensual experience of the golf swing to nothing more than angles and elbows. We call this the Pez Dispenser School of Golf—"Bend your knees, thirty bucks please"— talking heads spewing advice that has very little, if anything, to do with the person swinging the club. They believe in teaching you; we believe in having you learn. There is a big difference.

The conventional way of instruction is also a school of thought that creates a dependent relationship between the student and the teacher. We believe in the Socratic coaching method. We want you to learn to coach yourself by helping you to understand yourself better and by showing you how to draw out your own abilities. You are always with yourself on the golf course. What more reliable coach could you have?

Absolutely essential to our approach is the notion that you should only concern yourself with the things that are under your control. Not only should every shot have a purpose, but every action should have a purpose as well. And the purpose of golf is all about getting the ball in the hole—pure and simple. Why make the game any more complicated than that? There is a ton of truth in the old cliché: "They don't ask you how, they ask how many." **Don't waste energy fretting about those things over which you have no control. When you do that, all you are doing is borrowing trouble.**

To get the ball in the hole as efficiently as possible, you must channel your energies only toward those things you can influence. We call these things CONTROLLABLE GOALS. Score is not a controllable goal. Neither is winning. Bad bounces, bad weather, an opponent having a career day, and endless other things all take control out of your hands in regard to score and winning. You will learn how to develop a PLAYING FOCUS that will keep your mind centered on the task at hand—hitting the shot you are about to play.

What do we mean by PLAYING FOCUS? It includes things like preparation, focus, tempo, and commitment. How many times have you been playing well when a thought such as this crossed your mind: "Gee, if I play the last five holes two over par I can shoot my career-best round"? And how often is it the case that, almost as soon as you start adding up your score, the round falls apart? You have let your focus shift from the controllable—your PLAYING FOCUS—to the uncontrollable—your score.

Let's take practice as an example of an aspect of your game over which you have definite control. Many players spend a lot of time and energy on the practice range, hit the ball great there, and don't get any better when they take their game out on the course. That's because they practice in a context that has nothing to do with the game of golf. So much of teaching in this game is economically driven. Here's my twenty bucks, give me a bucket of balls. Scrape and hit, scrape and hit. Give myself a perfect lie and hit the shot. The balls are gone. I must be done practicing. **If you are going to practice, make it useful time, not time used up.**

A lot of players will wear blistered hands as a badge of honor showing how hard they have worked. But what was accomplished? Most players develop Golf Attention Deficit Disorder (GADD) because of a practice culture that teaches us to value quantity over quality. The practice of standing on the range hitting one hundred balls with little thought and no purpose is actually teaching your mind to be less focused on the golf course and it is encouraging your swing to be less disciplined. And you wonder why the player you are on the range is not the same player who shows up on the course! With our approach you will learn how to cultivate a PLAYING FOCUS on the range that works for you on the golf course.

Bobby Jones said there is golf and then there is tournament golf. He was right. There is also practice golf and real golf. We will show you how to integrate the two. Part of our message is that if you want to score better, simulate real golf when you practice. You will learn how to do this through simple drills and enjoyable games that will make your practice not only more productive but also more fun. You will also learn how to use the game's proving ground—the golf course—as a practice facility. The course should be not just a proving ground but a learning ground as well.

Most people practice by giving themselves a perfect lie and then hitting a dozen shots with the same club at the same target. How is that like real golf? How often do you do that on the golf course? How often in a round do you hit even two 8-irons in a row? Rarely, we hope! Switch clubs after every shot. Switch targets. If you are working on the takeaway, maybe you don't even need a ball in front of you. Just work on the takeaway. Ask yourself: What's my INTENTION? And then ask: Am I paying ATTENTION to that? When you practice you should be grooving not only your swing but also your mind.

Take putting as another example. Why do people practice by putting with three balls to one target? Is that the way you do it on the course? Why not practice with one ball to a different hole each time? Why not practice your putting by chipping and then putting, the way you would on a course? Why not simulate the pressure you experience on the golf course in practice by saying you want to make up-and-down five consecutive times before you stop practicing? Make your brain recalibrate after every shot. That is far more important to a productive practice session than the number of balls you hit or the number of hours you put in.

The traditional way of practicing makes you better on the range, but it does not transfer to the course because it has nothing to do with the reality of golf. **Remember, every shot must have a purpose, even in practice.** That is where the habit of good golf is formed. **That is where you learn what you can trust, and develop trust in what you have learned.**

The most common cry we hear from golfers of all skill levels is that they want to be more consistent. By paying more attention to your practice and to the way you perform on the golf course, you will discover that you are more consistent than you think. It is one definition of insanity to keep doing the same thing with no success but to continue to repeat the process hoping for a different outcome. It is also the action of

a person who is not paying ATTENTION to his INTEN-
TION. Remember, our worst tendencies show up under
pressure. Pay attention. Take notes. Write them down. Do the
same when you play your best golf. Try to understand what is
going on and how you are feeling when you play well. Your
consistency lies in the fact that you mess up in the same ways
and you succeed in the same ways. Learn to recognize both
and learn to understand both. Call it golf therapy. To do this
you will need to discard some of what you have been taught
about golf. **You will need to empty your head so wisdom can flow in.**

As you must have clear intentions in order to become a
better golfer, so we must have clear intentions to become better teachers. Here are the beliefs we bring to our coaching:

- Each human is unique.
- Each human has unlimited potential.
- Distinguish between who you are and what you do.
- Golf is a game to be played.
- Developing balance is essential.
- Performance is about getting the ball in the hole.
- No one is broken. Every human being can develop.
- The physical, technical, mental, emotional, and social parts
  of golf and life are integrated.
- Learning is a lifetime process.

That's who we are. Now, let's start to learn more about
who you are by asking yourself these questions:

- If you could be any golfer in the world, who would you like to be?
- When did you show the most courage ever?
- What is the best golf shot you ever hit?
- If golf could be even more fun, how would that be?
- What's the thing you are best at?
- What is the one thing you are most proud of in your golf?
- What's the most fun you have ever had on a golf course?

In more than two decades of working with players of all skill levels—from beginners to those playing professionally—we have found some startlingly similar signposts that lead to success. A successful golf swing is not always a pretty golf swing. A successful golf swing is one that repeats, especially under pressure. And nothing sabotages a golf swing more successfully than tension, those times when you grip the club too tightly or swing too fast or just get so angry you can't think straight. Tension comes from fear, and fear comes from a lack of confidence and a loss of trust. You will learn how to find that trust in your abilities, and how to rediscover it when it seems to be slipping away.

We've all had that experience of standing over a golf shot and feeling absolutely certain in our heart of hearts that the ball is going to follow the flight we imagine in our minds. And we have also all had the feeling of standing over a shot afraid to start the backswing because we feel that we have no idea where the ball is going to go. Yet it's the same person holding the same club and bringing to the shot the same mechanics that have proven to work in the past.

What's the difference? Attitude. Actually, it is more than just attitude. It is perception and state of mind. That's what we are going to change in the following pages: how you approach the game and how you perceive the game. We will teach you how to practice with a purpose and how to play with a purpose. Through our approach—GOLF54—you will learn how to develop routines you can trust and how to transfer those routines from the range to the golf course. You will learn how to embrace your ability to achieve your ultimate potential.

Do you want to take your game from the driving range to the golf course? Do you want to see the hours of effort you put into practice result in lower scores on the golf course? Do you want to swing better? Do you want to think better on the golf course? Do you want better emotional control under pressure? Do you want to integrate all of this? Then GOLF54 is for you.

Why do we call our approach GOLF54? It is a philosophy Pia developed when she was head coach of the Swedish National Team, and Pia and Lynn have since expanded and refined it. While the cultural concern with fairness in Sweden produces good people, it does not promote the creation of peak-performance athletes. Pia found that Swedish golfers set their goals too low—and that low goals were exactly what they achieved. The only way to break out of this box of limited achievement is to set loftier expectations.

What would be the most outrageous goal in golf? How about eighteen consecutive birdies—a 54 on a par-72 course. Traditional thinking says, "That's impossible. How can anyone shoot 54?" But progress is always a break with tradition. It is a paradigm shift. We say: **Imagine the impossible, and then figure out how to make it happen.** You are capable of hitting a perfect shot—you've done it. You will learn how to string those shots together. You will learn how to have your own VISION54.

One of the players on Pia's Swedish National Team was a promising young woman named Annika Sorenstam. She was talented but shy, the perfect model of the Swedish athlete who wanted success but shunned the spotlight that comes with it. Her shyness and determination, however, became the perfect breeding ground for big dreams. Most comfortable in her solitude, she brilliantly built walls against the distractions around her and focused on the game of golf.

With a passion sometimes mistaken for aloofness, Sorenstam looked inside and found the focus that allowed her to maximize her potential on the golf course, eventually becoming the first woman to shoot 59 in an LPGA event and the first woman in fifty-eight years to play in a PGA Tour event. Annika is the embodiment of the spirit of GOLF54. She sets lofty goals and then devises strategies to realize them. She understands that the impossible is merely the stringing together of the possible. And she is one of the absolute best at focusing only on the things she can control.

"I think it's possible to shoot 54," Sorenstam says. "Birdie Number one, birdie Number two, birdie Number three. I believe you can hit every fairway, I believe you can hit every green, and why not one putt? That makes a 54. Try to make it as simple as possible."

How does such an audacious goal relate to the average golfer? Well, it speaks to the nagging question asked by everyone, from the occasional recreational player to the committed professional: "If I can hit one good shot, why can't I hit two in a row? If I can play one hole well, why can't I play eighteen holes well? If I can play one round well, why can't I play well every time out?"

We say there is absolutely no reason why that cannot be the case. GOLF54 will put you more in touch with your ability so you can approach your ultimate potential. For some, such as Annika, that potential includes a 54. For others it means a more reliable—and more enjoyable—experience on the golf course. Next time you see Annika playing, look at the headcover on her 7-wood. It is a knit cover in the blue and yellow of the Swedish flag with the number 54 on it. It is to remind Annika to keep VISION54 in her focus. We believe we can teach you your own VISION54.

When Ben Hogan, the person most people say invented practice, was asked the key to his success as a golfer, he liked to say, "The secret is in the dirt." But we think old Ben was holding out on everyone. When Hogan practiced, it was always with a purpose. When he played it was always with a passion. No one was ever more prepared for a competitive round than Hogan was, and few have had as much trust in their routine as Hogan. That trust was formulated long before he stepped to the first tee.

Hogan used to warm up for each competitive round by hitting the shots in the order he was going to hit them on the golf course. Once, a few weeks before the 1951 U.S. Open, a friend came upon Hogan practicing by himself at his home course in Texas, hitting knockdown 150-yard 5-irons. When asked what he was doing, Hogan replied: "I'm going to need that shot at Oakland Hills." Yes, practice will make you better, but only if you practice the right things and approach practice in the right way—only if you practice with a purpose, only if you play with a purpose. The secret is not in the dirt, it is in you. We'll help you find it.

CHAPTER II

Change Your Brain to Change Your Game

"If you think you can, you can. And if you think you can't, you're right."

—HENRY FORD, TWENTIETH-CENTURY
AMERICAN INVENTOR

SWING KEY: Bad swings lead to bad shots, but it is often bad thoughts that lead to bad swings.

Patty Sheehan, the LPGA Hall of Fame player, was playing the final hole of a tournament when she needed to hit a fairway wood second shot to a green protected by water on a par-5 hole. A birdie was essential to stay in contention, and the possibility of an eagle was a chance she had to take. What resulted, however, was her worst swing of the day—in fact, probably one of the worst swings she ever made in competition—and she cold topped the shot. As the ball bounded down the fairway and into the creek short of the green, she watched her chances of winning disappear with it.

The shocked television commentators said, "Let's take a look at what happened here," and they ran slow-motion replays that showed a reverse pivot and that Sheehan had come right out of the shot, leading to the top. But the TV commentators missed the point. If they wanted to run a meaningful replay they should have shown tape of the indecision BEFORE Sheehan hit the shot. First she had her hand on a fairway wood, then she stepped away from the ball and her caddie handed her an iron. Then she went back to the fairway wood. The indecision in the shot selection led to a lack of commitment during the shot. The poor swing resulted from poor thinking.

The way most players would react after hitting a shot like that is to go to the practice range and hit that fairway wood over and over again. It would be a complete waste of time and energy. Sheehan could hit that shot a thousand times on the range and still mess it up next time she had to perform it under pressure. To see that bad shot as a swing problem is to view golf as merely a mechanical game. It is a much more beautiful sport than that.

What happens when we fail to perform when it matters most? The answer is simultaneously complicated and simple. It's complicated because it involves more than just the swing, and it is simple for the same reason. Every student who comes to us has one clear goal: They want to get the ball in the hole in fewer strokes. We love the challenge as coaches to help the player figure out a way that works best for them. And we know from experience that the journey ends up being different for everyone who plays the game. Think of VISION54 as a metaphor for your goal, your dream round of golf. Then think of GOLF54 as a way to achieve your goal. The mistake the TV commentators made was in focusing on Sheehan's poor swing and not understanding that the poor swing was not the disease but the symptom. Like most golfers—and most teachers—the commentators were obsessed with the mechanical aspect of the game, and that is only a small part of the road to success.

Playing the game involves many components, and the great players figure that out. It all starts with imagination and then matures into a plan to make the vision happen. Jack Nicklaus once finished a round with which he was not happy and immediately headed to the practice range. He took a ball out of the bucket, placed it at his feet, and stood over the ball, arms folded, staring down at it. After several minutes of staring at the ball Nicklaus said to his caddie, "I've got it," and left the range without ever hitting a shot. The next day he shot a 65 and won the tournament. Jack knew that the game is more than the mechanical act of swinging the club. He was looking for something else when he stared at that ball—and he knew it was there. He understood that golf has many components and that the component he was missing that day was not in his swing alone.

We like to break golf down to these five elements: Physical, Technical, Mental, Emotional, and Social. All five influence how you score. All five need to be looked at if you want to realize your potential. If any of the five areas is not in your field of awareness, your potential is compromised. Instead of focusing so completely on the TECHNICAL aspect of the 3-wood Sheehan hit, the commentators would have spent their time more usefully by looking at her MENTAL preparation for that shot or her EMOTIONAL state when she made the swing. They, like many instructors, were trying to fix a bad shot by honing in on the swing, when in fact the poor swing likely resulted from a lack of commitment to the shot or poor focus.

If a scientist were trying to sum up our teaching approach in an equation, it would be simply this:

$$P+T+M+E+S=54$$

We describe the five elements this way:

Physical: This includes fitness, posture, nutrition, proper rest, proper warm-up, etc.

Technical: This includes the swing, grip, stance, aim, fundamentals, ball and club fitting, shot-making ability, etc.

Mental: This includes your focus, motivation, decision making, how you talk to yourself, goal setting, strategy, etc.

Emotional: This includes your feelings and what you can do about them. Are you nervous, angry, anxious, over-excited? Do you have a passion for the game?

Social: This includes your interaction with others, such as playing partners, the slow group in front of you, family, coach, caddie, etc.

Think about yourself. Which of these elements or areas do you focus on? What are you good at in each area? What can be better? Awareness is a key to good golf, and awareness requires honesty. Ask someone close to you evaluate you in each area. Compare their perception of you to your own. Do you have difficulty making decisions or fulfilling a commitment? Are you easily angered or frightened? Do you let the actions of a playing partner or opponent distract you? Do you warm up properly before a round and rest well the night before? Do you really care about playing better golf and are you willing to commit to that feeling?

Unfortunately, many players and teachers focus only on the Technical and maybe the Physical. Both are important but are far from the whole picture. And it is very easy to be tricked into thinking you have a swing problem when that is not the case. If your Physical, Mental, Emotional, or Social is weak it shows up in the swing, but it does not mean that your technical swing is the problem. If a player feels fear standing over the ball, it might make the muscles tighten and result in a swing that is too fast or a pivot that never gets completed. The critical issue is: What should the player go practice?

If you only go to the range to work on making a better turn or slowing your tempo, you are working on a symptom and not a cause. This is where honesty comes into play. The first step toward expanding our perception of the game in general and reaching a better understanding of our own game in particular is to face reality. If that bad swing was caused because you tensed up under pressure, hitting a million practice balls won't fix the problem. **Bad swings lead to bad shots, but it's often bad thoughts that lead to bad swings.**

If you want to play to your full ability, you must recognize that you are a mind, a body, and a heart. You must admit that you experience emotions as you play and recognize that you have relationships in the culture of golf, just as you do in your life. You don't experience golf in a vacuum unless you choose to always play alone. You don't need to be Dr. Phil to figure out that an integrated approach—in which all aspects of the human experience are considered—is the most effective and most powerful method of human growth. If you learn to spot the five elements—P+T+M+E+S—in your own game, you can more easily appreciate them and use them to accelerate your own growth to a deeper way of being. And yes, you will shoot lower scores!

Clearly, what we are asking you to do is to think differently about the game. If you understand all five of golf's components and believe that you can make yourself a better player by learning to better control those components, that will be the case. We are asking you not only to expand your understanding of the game but also to increase your expectations for yourself. We believe it is possible to birdie every hole, which on a par-72 course would be a 54. Why have we latched onto such an audacious notion? **Because essential to our approach is the notion that WHAT WE BELIEVE, WE BECOME.** What we think, speak, and act becomes the foundation for our future. Our brains are wired for beliefs and expectations. We have virtually unlimited human potential to cultivate, but too often we let the memory of failure and the negative thoughts of those around us reduce those expectations. We believe that by pursuing golf—and life—with the intention of 54, you can create a climate for excellence.

The beliefs we have about ourselves influence how well we perform. If we think golf is difficult and that two putts per green is acceptable, we have wired our brain/body for this to be true. The world is full of perceived limitations that stop us from developing our potential and from being as great as we are. Our culture, our sport, and our families have embedded a belief system in us that influences what we think is possible. These beliefs greatly influence our attitudes, awareness, and self-esteem.

If we have unlimited potential how do we get there? We like to say, "Imagine the impossible and then figure out how to make it happen." What would it take to birdie every hole? How would we practice to prepare ourselves to shoot 54? How would we think? How would we manage our emotions? How would we eat, sleep, and drink? How fit do we need to be? What shots do we need to learn? What attitude do we need to stay committed to? What tools do we need to coach ourselves physically, mentally, and emotionally? Albert Einstein said that he came up with his theory of general relativity by imagining what he would see if he were riding on a beam of light at the speed of light. He imagined the impossible, and then he explained it.

During Pia's first year as head coach in Sweden with the Swedish National Team, she realized that many of the players held limiting beliefs about themselves and the game. The players from junior level to professional would often be heard saying, "How can we be great golfers coming from a country where the summers are so short, the winters so long, the greens so bad?"

These players were part of the "lagom" culture and were not daring to be great. Swedes often use the word *lagom*—which means "just enough"—as an expression of approval for many things. Lagom derives from Viking times, when a large container of beer was passed around a table to drink. So that no one should drink too much, "lagom" was regularly uttered. This showed consideration for the last person to drink by making sure there was enough beer left. Such thoughtfulness has survived, and today lagom is the perfect description of many aspects of Swedish culture. Lagom is great for many things but not for realizing one's unique potential and peak performance.

In 1991, Pia, together with Kjell Enhager, the author of the book *Quantum Golf,* presented the players with the concept of VISION54. They convinced the players that this wild notion was possible by having them think about rounds they had played on their home course. At one time or another they had made a birdie on every hole on the course. So why not make all eighteen of those birdies on one day? Now they could see that it was possible. They just hadn't done it during the same round . . . yet! And so VISION54 was born.

Pia was ridiculed a lot in the early days of VISION54. Golf's governing bodies were not supportive of someone doing that to "old man par." A question we often get today is, "If you can shoot 54, what about 53?" This question misses the secret.

Yes, 54 is a SCORE, but what it truly represents is a PRO-CESS for human beings to stay curious about their potential and to remain open to continuous learning. Another confusion people often make with the 54 is staying attached to it during the process. **You can't make the 54 happen, but you can stay committed to a process that can make it possible.** The COMMITMENT to the INTENTION of 54 is the secret.

Wherever you are in life and golf you can create your own 54 to inspire and light the way.

Dare to be as good as you are.
Believe in the potential of yourself and others.
Stay open to possibilities.
And remember, your past is not your future.

Bold visions push the boundaries of what is possible. Perhaps the only limits to human potential are the limits of our imagination and our commitment.

54 . . . Expect More!

CHAPTER III

Think Inside the Box

"The future belongs to those who prepare for it."
—RALPH WALDO EMERSON, NINETEENTH-CENTURY
AMERICAN AUTHOR

SWING KEY: Decide, commit, swing. It's as simple as that.

One of the true joys of being a sports fan—no matter the sport—is experiencing those rare moments when a great athlete becomes even better. One phrase used to refer to this phenomenon is "being in the zone." Truly, what occurs is a transcendent experience in which the body and mind seamlessly merge into one and the functioning of the physical self is not interfered with by the mental self. Concentration is complete, commitment is total, and the result at times defies comprehension. The temptation would be to say that at these moments someone becomes better than he really is, when in fact what is happening is that someone is allowing himself to reach his full potential. Athletes at times refer to this state by saying, "I got out of my own way," a very telling phrase.

Athletes who have performed at this supreme level have a startling similarity in how they describe the feeling, detailing what amounts to an out-of-body experience. When Bill Walton made twenty-one of twenty-two shots in a college basketball championship game, he said he saw the action unfolding a half-second before the reality revealed itself to others on the court. The great football running back Jim Brown described the sensation of running toward where he anticipated a hole would be in the line only to have the hole magically appear right as he got there. And when Al Geiberger became the first PGA Tour player to shoot a 59 in competition, he said he never considered that he might miss critical putts over the last few holes, describing the cup as appearing to be the size of a garbage can.

In each of these cases the action was not impeded by thought. The body, while trying to perform a complicated physical action, was not encumbered by decision making. If Walton or Brown had taken the fraction of a second to think about their moves before making them, the moves would have come too late and would have been thwarted. If Geiberger had been thinking about shooting 59 rather than being lost in the moment of the shot he was about to hit, he never would have recorded that magical round. The key is not that these athletes shut off their minds, but rather that their mental preparation was so complete and their belief in that preparation so total that they were able to perform with absolute trust. The physical did not so much transcend the mental as it merged with it.

How can we achieve this level of performance more often on the golf course? There is no greater saboteur of the golf swing than tension. And there is no greater creator of tension than a lack of confidence in your ability to perform the task you are about to undertake. At the absolute center of a golf game you can trust there must be a routine you can believe in. This is no different from any other area of your life. It is the entering and exiting of rooms that creates tension in us. The time we spend in those rooms eventually becomes a matter of ease because we have established a routine pattern of behavior with which we are comfortable. When we step up to hit a golf shot, we must be in a room where doubt and fear are not allowed.

How do we create this room? Well, of all the thousands of instruction aids that are on the market—from harnesses and straps to other bells and whistles—the most important training device you ever purchase could very well be a one-cent piece of yarn about three feet long. Here is what we want you to do. Place a ball on the ground at the practice range. Behind the ball about a yard (allowing you enough room to take your stance at the ball), attach the piece of yarn to the ground with two tees perpendicular to the intended line of flight of the shot. Now, stand behind the string with your shoulders square to the target. You are now in the THINK BOX.

Take a step across the yarn and take your stance at the ball. This is the PLAY BOX. All decisions are made in the THINK

BOX. When you cross that line, which we call the DECISION LINE (when you are on the golf course, it will be an imaginary line), QUIT THINKING and PLAY.

As you stand in the THINK BOX you should consider all the variables for the shot: wind direction and strength, the lie of the ball (is it below your feet and will it thus fade away from your body?), the hazards you need to factor in, and, if you are in competition, the point at which you stand in the match. VERBALIZE to yourself your intentions for the shot. "I am going to hit a 6-iron at the tree behind the left corner of the green and the ball will fade toward the pin in the back right corner of the green. It is a good, firm 6-iron for me." Imagine the shot you are going to hit.

The only time there is any indecision should be when you are in the THINK BOX. When you cross the DECISION LINE to hit the shot, there must be total commitment to the shot. If you get over the ball and are not comfortable with the decision you have made, back off, retreat to the THINK BOX, and come up with a plan in which you have trust. If you are going to be slow in any part of the game, it must be in the THINK BOX and not in the PLAY BOX. The DECISION LINE is the doorway from one room to another. When you cross the line into the PLAY BOX, leave doubt behind, make your grip, aim the club face, align the body, connect to the target, and hit your shot. The longer you wait to hit the shot the more opportunity there is for doubt—and tension—to creep into your mind and body. And remember what we said about tension being the most effective saboteur of the golf swing. *Decide, commit, swing. It's as simple as that.*

THE THINK BOX

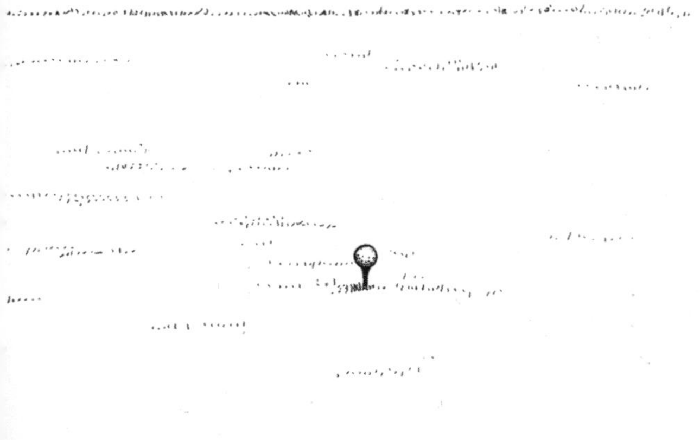

THE PLAY BOX

Understanding the THINK BOX/PLAY BOX is all about learning the process of playing the game. As we said in the previous chapter, the swing is just one piece of the puzzle. The other components are all part of the games within the game that comprise the game. Being aware of the THINK BOX/PLAY BOX is something you can practice while you are playing. Remember, the golf course is not only a proving ground but also a learning ground. In fact, it is your most important learning ground. The more you understand the way you behave on the golf course, the more rapidly your play will improve.

Let's take a closer look at what lies on either side of the DECISION LINE.

THINK BOX

It is analytical, left brain, digital, intellectual. This is where you consider the yardage, analyze the lie, consider the shot options, make the club selection, take the wind into consideration, analyze what the ball will do when it lands (kick left or right, etc.), decide on your swing thought, and make your practice swing. These are mostly external factors, but you should also be checking internally to determine what shot you feel you can trust the most at this moment. You must be honest with yourself in the THINK BOX. This can change from day to day. We are dynamic, changing human beings, and the right decision today may not be the right decision tomorrow.

PLAY BOX

It is sensory, right brain, involves imagery and analogue, is instinctual. Develop some connection between yourself and the target. Some just grip it and rip it. Some hum a song. Others say they hear the target speaking to them. Still others imagine the swing path and the ball flight as it hones in on the target. The PLAY BOX is about feel—soft hands, a low center of gravity. To be lost in the flow and headed for peak performance there can be no digital thinking in the PLAY BOX.

We like people to develop the most efficient routine possible. Playing great golf over a period of time is a lot about energy management. If you are not sure why you are doing something in the THINK BOX, take it out! Some players decide to keep practice swings, and some decide to quit making them. The THINK BOX doesn't need to be the slow box. In fact, part of energy management is being efficient—and decisive—in the THINK BOX. Think of it as skydiving. In the THINK BOX you pack your parachute, pick the jump site, and do all the other preparations. In the PLAY BOX you just jump.

We never know in golf if we make the right decisions, but we need to make a bunch every time we hit a shot, and we need to learn how to stick with the decisions we make. We have seen many swings technically improve just by the player making more committed decisions. Certainly, we have all seen the "steer job" swing when someone has not totally committed to the shot and, because of lack of confidence, makes a swing in which he or she tries to "guide" the ball into the fairway. That always leads to trouble. And again, the bad swing did not result from poor technique, but rather the poor technique resulted from flaws in the mental or emotional side of the GOLF54 equation.

After crossing the DECISION LINE into the PLAY BOX,

nothing matters but the target. Step up to the ball; focus your attention on the target and let go of everything else. The PLAY BOX is not the place to second-guess your swing or any decisions you made in the THINK BOX. Here, you should just swing the club and execute your shot. Making this little ritual part of your routine increases the odds of your ball landing where you want it to land.

Annika Sorenstam gave a great example of the importance of her routine on Saturday in the 2004 U.S. Women's Open at The Orchards in Massachusetts. She came to a short par-4 dogleg to the right and grabbed her 4-wood, put her ball on the tee, and then looked up to see that the group in front had not cleared the fairway yet. Instead of letting the delay disrupt her routine, Annika took the ball off the tee, took the tee out of the ground, put the 4-wood back in the bag and put the headcover back on the 4-wood. Instead of standing in the PLAY BOX letting second thoughts creep into her mind— and perhaps getting angry about the delay—she retreated to the THINK BOX to mentally reload. This is the kind of discipline that has made Annika the great player she is. Tiger Woods has similar discipline. Ever notice how many times he has actually stopped a swing and stepped away from a shot? That takes enormous mental commitment.

The best golfers in the world have access to both sides of their brain and body. They can be creative, intuitive, calm, aware of details, perceptive of their emotional state, and able to analyze the course, construct an appropriate strategy, and keep the big picture and its possibilities in mind. The balance between the left and the right has to do with the balance between being aware of details and being aware of the whole. It's about your ability to be both creative and logical. It's about the physical balance between the left and right halves of the body. The right half of the brain controls and is stimulated by the left side of the body, and the left half of the brain controls and is stimulated by the right side of the body. Harmony is achieved by integration.

We believe that golf is both a science and an art. There is no better example of this than Tiger Woods. He has enormous physical skills and is brilliant at course management, but he is also a player of extreme imagination and startling feel and creativity. It was his ability to be in touch with both sides of his brain and his body that enabled him to continue to be successful even when his game was less than it should have been because he was going through a swing change following knee surgery. While his technical side was in turmoil, Woods managed to draw even more on his emotional and mental side.

All decisions are made in the THINK BOX. All action unfolds in the PLAY BOX. The delicious irony here is that by drawing a DECISION LINE between the physical and the mental—in the case of the piece of yarn, we have quite literally done that—we have enabled these sometimes competing components of our self to merge. As with anything we do in life, we will do it more successfully if we attack the endeavor with complete trust in our plan of action. While the golf swing is a lot about rhythm, the most successful way to achieve that rhythm is to slow down the mental and to speed up the physical. Take the time to plan the shot and waste no time hitting the shot.

Meg Mallon, a two-time U.S. Women's Open champion, said of Annika Sorenstam: "I hope young players and their coaches notice that the best player in the world is also the fastest player in the world." What Meg means is that when Annika steps up to hit a shot there is not an elaborate, time-consuming series of waggles and false takeaways and repetitive looks at the target before she swings. All of the doubt embodied in those indecisive movements has been left in the THINK BOX. When you cross the DECISION LINE, it is time to PLAY. That's when the fun begins.

CHAPTER IV

Think Small, Play Big

"Only those who risk going too far can possibly find out how far one can go."

 —T.S. ELIOT, TWENTIETH-CENTURY AMERICAN WRITER

SWING KEY: Play each shot as if it will only happen once.

While anticipation is one of the most compelling of human emotions, inertia is the most relentless of physical forces. Too many times, the joy we get from imagining what a goal achieved will feel like turns into disappointment when we allow that ambition to be reduced to a mere daydream. When we let ourselves get stuck in our lives we are surrendering to the strongest of natural forces—the instinctual urge to resist change. The laws of inertia say that a body at rest tends to stay at rest unless acted on by an outside force, and that a body in motion tends to stay in motion unless acted on by an outside force. We have to learn how to become our own outside force.

Big goals are achieved by thinking small. That's true in golf just as it is in everything else. Again, the key to playing better golf is in treating it not as a mechanical activity that is apart from the whole human, but rather as an action that is a part of the expression of who you are as a person. It is a ballet with clubs and golf balls. Everyone doesn't have to swing the golf club the same way. There is more than one right way to swing a club, but there is only one you. One of the first steps toward better golf for any of us is to realize who we are and how that matches up with what we are trying to achieve. Another initial step—and perhaps the most crucial—is to accept that like anything else in our lives, what we can achieve is limited primarily by what we believe we can achieve.

We like to say: "IMAGINE THE IMPOSSIBLE, AND THEN FIGURE OUT HOW TO MAKE IT HAPPEN." That's what GOLF54 is all about. The impossible is merely a stringing together of the possible. Perfection is a series of achievable tasks performed so seamlessly that their simplicity is lost in the enormity of the accomplishment. How can someone make eighteen consecutive birdies? It's simple: Hit one fairway. Hit one green. Make one putt. Do that eighteen times. It is a seemingly impossible task when looked at as a whole, but when broken down into its components, it suddenly crosses the line into the realm of the possible. The focus needed to pursue eighteen consecutive birdies is the same as the focus needed to pursue eighteen consecutive pars or eighteen consecutive bogeys, if that is the next stage in your development as a player. Remember, VISION54 is FOCUS on whatever YOUR dream is. The key to that focus is training your mind to concentrate on the achievable in order to give yourself the opportunity to do the unimaginable.

Energy conservation is not just an environmental problem, it is an emotional problem. Energy should only be expended on CONTROLLABLE GOALS. Sure, maybe we can't fight City Hall, but we can determine the people who run it. Tilting at windmills achieves nothing, but building a sail to catch the breeze can take us to places unimaginable. It's all about focus. It's all about what you can accomplish. It's all about identifying controllable goals and then developing a plan to achieve them.

What can you control on the golf course and what is out of your control? This is the same as asking: Where should your PLAYING FOCUS be centered? In both practice and play, the focus must remain only on those things that are within your control. In sports psychology terms, we are setting process goals instead of outcome goals. In reality what we are doing is establishing an INTENTION that gives us direction and focus.

To reach your greatest potential as a golfer (and a human being), start investigating what elements of the game you can and can't control. For example, you might let yourself get frustrated by things like bad weather, questionable pin placements, or bad etiquette by someone in your group. This is a complete waste of time and a needless expenditure of emotional energy, since these are all things you can't do anything about anyway. Instead, focus your energy on parts of the game you can influence, like your pre-shot routine, warm-up, strategy, and club selection.

The ability to focus on what you can control and let go of what you can't is very important in tournament golf. Both Annika Sorenstam and Maria Hjorth have won LPGA tournaments after losing or damaging their clubs just before the start of an event. In both cases, the players consciously decided to focus on what they could do with their newly borrowed clubs. Had they reacted the way most of us would have in that situation—with self-pity and frustration—they would have missed the cut before teeing off. Similarly, at the 1999 British Open the Carnoustie course was set up to be extremely difficult. Before the tournament started, during practice rounds, one top player after another complained about the playing conditions. You could virtually make a list of which players had lost the tournament even before it began. It is not surprising that two players who never complained— Jean Van de Velde and eventual winner Paul Lawrie—played the best that week. They knew they could not control the playing conditions, but they could control their attitude about them.

Here is a drill to do the next time you play. Rate yourself on a scale from 1 to 10 on how well you take responsibility for the factors under your control. Give yourself lower points when you waste energy on things you can't do anything about, and then tally up your score at the end of the round. Try to raise that number every time you play. Here are some things you can score yourself on in both categories.

YOU CAN CONTROL
Your temper
Your equipment
Your warm-up
Pre-shot routine
Post-shot routine
Pre-swing fundamentals
Aiming
Your attitude
Your club selection
Your strategy
Decision and commitment
Your diet
Your posture
Your own speed of play

YOU CAN'T CONTROL
The weather
Your playing partners
Others' speed of play
Pin placement
Course conditions
Score
Breaks
Lies
Tee times
Past shots
Winning

Everyone who plays the game of golf has a dream of what they want to accomplish. That is a GOAL. It might be winning the U.S. Open, winning your club championship, breaking 100, or getting your handicap down to single digits. It is very important to have these future goals and to keep on dreaming. But it is essential to have a PLAYING FOCUS that brings your mind back to the present, thinking about one shot at a time and focused on something that you can control. That is your INTENTION, your plan to achieve your goal, which gives you direction toward it. Competition is a good thing, but it is how you deal with competition and the mind-set you adopt to stay in the present when you compete that are important. **Play each shot as if it will only happen once.**

Winning the tournament or shooting a specific score is a great goal, but it is one that lies in your future and is actually not under your control. What is in the present—the now—is your act of swinging the club or stroking the putt. To do this successfully, you need to have access to all of your abilities. To have access to all of your abilities, you need to be in the present, hitting your golf shots. We spend a lot of our time as coaches teaching players how to be in the NOW as they are hitting the shot, and not lost somewhere in the future or past.

One tool to refine focus is to have "a game within the game." This is a drill that helps develop a PLAYING FOCUS, or what sports psychologists would call a process goal. For this to work, the PLAYING FOCUS needs to be your main focus while on the course. The PLAYING FOCUS keeps you in the game, keeps you engaged. By committing to your PLAY-

ING FOCUS you give yourself the best chance of scoring well and of achieving your future goal. While the commitment to the PLAYING FOCUS must be total, the focus itself can change from day to day. To help players remain committed to their PLAYING FOCUS, we have them keep their own PLAYING FOCUS scorecard. The act of recording a score for how well you did with your personal playing focus on every shot is a tool of accountability.

The PLAYING FOCUS score can be a rating from 1 (low) to 5 (high). The secret to this game within the game is staying committed to your PLAYING FOCUS regardless of outcome. What we have witnessed is that players will scrap a PLAYING FOCUS if it isn't producing the score or result they want. It's this type of short-term thinking that pulls players into the failures of the past or the illusions of the future rather than focusing on the shot at hand.

HERE ARE SOME EXAMPLES OF DIFFERENT TYPES OF PLAYING FOCUS:

Today after every shot I will react with a happy or neutral state.

On every shot I will make a clear decision and have the guts to go through with the decision.

I will maintain my balance today in my finish position an extra five seconds.

I will do my pre-shot routine on every shot for all eighteen holes.

I will make my post-shot routine positive.

I will take an extra deep breath in my pre-shot routine.
Once I have taken my grip in the THINK BOX, I will keep
my hand pressure constant.

The criteria for a successful PLAYING FOCUS is that it
must be stated POSITIVELY (don't say: "I will not leave any
putts short today." Instead say, "I will get the ball past the hole
today"). It must be something that is UNDER YOUR CON-
TROL (don't say: "I want to shoot 65 and win the tournament," say, "I will remain committed to my decisions today").
It must also be SPECIFIC enough that you can score its
progress and stay accountable to it on every shot (not vague
like, "I will be consistent today," but rather, "I will maintain
my balance on every shot today").

Tiger Woods has this to say: "My creative mind is my
greatest weapon. It is a kind of inner-vision that enables me
to see things that others might not, like a certain way to play a
shot. It is the game within the game. I developed my mental
game early. I cannot overemphasize the importance of you
developing yours now."

Among the things we can control is total commitment to
each shot. For players of any level, but especially for the recreational golfer, it is easy to fall into the routine of hitting shots
and not thinking about shots. We develop that tendency in
the way we practice (the "scrape-and-hit" practice method
will be discussed later) and then we carry it with us out onto
the golf course. Have you ever hit a shot that went astray and
as you were walking to the next shot—usually well off line—
you have this conversation with yourself: "What was I think-

ing of there? I don't even remember hitting that ball." It is all too easy to let the line between the THINK BOX and the PLAY BOX disappear.

Here is a game to play to help develop that commitment to each shot. Play a round of golf using this scoring system: Give yourself one point for each fairway you hit, one point for each green you hit in regulation, one point for a par, two points for a birdie, and one point for each up-and-down you make—even if it is for a bogey or a double bogey or more. This game will help teach you that every shot must have a purpose by giving every shot a value. The fact that something is at stake with each swing—more than the uncontrollable goal of your final score—will help you keep your mind in the now. When you are in the THINK BOX you will be focused on the point at stake and you will develop a plan of action to gain that point. That plan of action is your INTENTION. When you step into the PLAY BOX you will have that plan of action and the belief that the plan will succeed.

When Annika Sorenstam shot the only 59 ever in an LPGA event, she started with eight consecutive birdies and allowed thoughts of her final score to creep into her head. After she finally made a par she had to refocus her thoughts on staying in the present and committing to clear decisions on every shot and maintaining the total courage to go through with those decisions. In talking about the round later, she spoke with a matter-of-fact calm about the accomplishment. Like a mountain climber who completely trusts in her equipment, putting her life in the integrity of the ropes and pegs and hooks, Annika believed in her preparation for her historic round. She regained her balance by getting back into her process thinking. She told herself, "No fear of consequences." That mantra allowed the birdies to start flowing again.

"The first time I broke 100, I was nervous," Sorenstam said later. "And I was nervous the first time I broke 90, 80, and 70. I was nervous the first time I broke 60, but I won't be the next time."

In many ways it is much like the psychological barrier that was shattered when Dr. Roger Bannister became the first person to run a mile in under four minutes. Once he did it a slew of other people followed. While only a handful of professional golfers have broken 60 in competition, the point is that perfection is achieved one shot at a time, and that the first step toward perfection is the belief that it is possible. Part of what makes great players great players is that, instead of imposing limits on what they think they can achieve, they challenge the concept of limits. And the key to challenging the concept of limits is to not limit your concept of success. The impossible dream is achieved through focus on controllable goals.

The surest way for a 15-handicap to guarantee a disappointing day on the golf course is to tee off thinking, "Today I am going to break 80." There is a way for that player to break 80, but the first notion has to be this: "I am going to get a point for putting this drive in the fairway," and to have a PLAYING FOCUS directed at that goal.

When Tiger Woods won the 2000 U.S. Open by an astounding 15 strokes at Pebble Beach, he hit many remarkable shots, but one of the most amazing is one of the most overlooked because it came well after the outcome of the tournament was decided. On the sixteenth hole of Sunday's final round, and in a position where Woods could have played the last three holes with only a putter and probably still won, he hit his approach shot over the green. The pin was on the back of the green, which was sloping away from Woods. There was no chance that he could chip the shot close to the hole.

Sure enough, Woods's pitch rolled about eighteen feet past the cup, leaving a difficult putt to make a par. In the grand scheme of things the putt was meaningless. He could three-putt and still have a double-digit lead. Yet Woods stalked the putt from all sides as if the outcome of the tournament was at stake, and when he finally stroked the ball into the hole to save par, Tiger responded with that trademark fist pump that usually accompanies only his most dramatic shots. Asked later why he studied that putt so carefully and reacted so emphatically when it found the bottom of the cup, Woods had a very telling answer.

"My goal for today's round was to make no bogies," he said. "With such a big lead [he was nine ahead starting the final round] I knew it would be difficult keeping my mind in the game, and once you let your concentration slip you lose control of what can happen."

It was Tiger's own version of the point game: Put the ball in the fairway, put the ball on the green, put the ball in the hole. He did not set his sights on the uncontrollable—a specific score or winning—but rather established an INTEN-TION and never let his mind drift away from that task. But the point game in and of itself is not a controllable goal. We still need a PLAYING FOCUS—like concentrating on tempo, or takeaway, or commitment to decisions. Asked what he thought about to calm his nerves in the final round of the 1996 Masters when he came from six strokes to defeat Greg Norman, Nick Faldo said: "I concentrated on starting my downswing slowly." It was a very specific playing focus that kept his mind in the now.

Driving the ball into the fairway is a goal we can all achieve. Hitting a green in regulation is also an objective achievable by most who play the game, and certainly making an up-and-down or sinking a putt is well within our reach. No matter what your skill level, working on the point game will help you teach yourself how to focus your concentration on the most important shot in golf—the one you are hitting right now. The point game will help you develop the use of a PLAYING FOCUS. And no matter how you define success in terms of a round you play, you will have a much better chance of achieving that success by learning how to focus on controllable goals. **Remember, the only shot that matters is the one you are going to hit right now.**

CHAPTER V

The Most Important Shot in Golf Is This One

"Experience is not what happens to you, it is what you do with what happens to you."

—ALDOUS HUXLEY, TWENTIETH-CENTURY
ENGLISH WRITER

SWING KEY: Say it, mean it, do it.

Tom Watson once said about Jack Nicklaus: "Jack never hit an indifferent golf shot in his life." Certainly, one of the reasons Nicklaus was able to establish a record that lends him claim to the title of Greatest Golfer Ever is that he understood that the most important shot in golf is the next one, and he was always totally committed to hitting that next shot. One of Jack's skills that is sometimes underappreciated is the control with which he played the game. We tend to think

of Nicklaus as brutishly strong—which he was—but his ultimate success was established by the conservative way in which
he played the game. Jack was a fairways-and-greens player
who only shot a 65 when he had to. He made sure he never
beat himself.

Among the other things said about Nicklaus that demon-
strate the depth of his domination is this by Tom Weiskopf,
who said that on a Sunday: "Jack knew he was going to beat
you. You knew Jack was going to beat you, and Jack knew that
you knew that he was going to beat you." Nicklaus's attitude
was not arrogance but confidence. He had total belief in his
preparation for the task at hand. And again, Jack wore down
an opponent not so much by overwhelming him with birdies
as by outlasting him with pars. Jack picked up his points and
waited for the competition to make mistakes. Usually, it did.

Take a look at all of the great players—Nicklaus, Bobby
Jones, Ben Hogan, Tiger, Annika—and among the traits they
share is an ability to wait out the opposition. Jones called it,
"Playing against Old Man Par." Nick Faldo, who won six major championships compared to two by Greg Norman, despite
not being anywhere near as physically skilled as Norman, said:
"Golf is not about the quality of your good shots, it is about
the quality of your bad shots." You do not have to hit spectacular shots to succeed; you need to avoid spectacularly bad
ones. In fact, if you have to hit a lot of spectacular shots it
probably means you've hit too many bad shots that you need
to recover from. Certainly that is what we saw from Tiger in
much of 2003 and 2004.

Good shots breed good shots. That is something even the

most casual golfer has learned. We call it confidence. We call it getting on a roll. Nicklaus, Jones, Sorenstam, and Hogan all had a magical fifteenth club in their bag when they competed. They BELIEVED they were going to play well. Developing that depth of belief does not happen by accident. Developing a ROUTINE that you TRUST involves more than merely deciding on a routine, it requires the work necessary to make the routine part of the game you take out onto the golf course. It is as important to practice your routine as it is to practice your swing, because your routine can get you through on those days when your swing may not be all that you want it to be.

One of the themes that we return to many times in this book is the need for practice to resemble real golf. One of the reasons golfers—professionals as well as recreational players—can't take their games from the range to the course is that, in the current practice culture, they are two different experiences. Just as we try to unify the mental with the mechanical aspects of the game, we also must try to erase the line between practice and playing. We want to teach you to play when you practice and practice when you play. In the end, it all has to be about executing golf shots with total commitment when it matters most. To do this you have to learn that playing needs to be *process* focus and not *score* focus. This makes you play better by focusing your concentration and it transforms the playing ground into a learning ground, which will help you down the road.

One of the nice things about many of our drills is that they can be done while you are playing without interfering with the recreational experience for either you or those you are playing with. THINK BOX/PLAY BOX goes from the range to the course with you—only on the course, the piece of yarn is imaginary. You can play the POINT GAME silently with yourself, focusing your concentration without disturbing your playing partners. The following drill is best done with a playing partner who wants to participate in the exercise with you. You could do it playing by yourself or with playing partners who are not doing the exercise, but about the time you started talking to yourself they would begin to think that the frustrations of the game had finally pushed you over the edge.

The way we do this drill in our school is to have the class break up into twosomes. The purpose of this drill—as with the POINT GAME—is to make the THINK BOX/PLAY BOX an ingrained part of your playing routine. Each player in the twosome has to verbalize his or her decisions for each shot. Ask yourself: "Exactly what am I going to do with this shot?" And then share your decision with your playing partner. You can do this drill by yourself, but we do find that it works best when you state your decisions out loud. It seems to help the player commit to the shot. Amazingly, we have seen swings improve when players started verbalizing their decisions for their shots. Some of the professionals we work with continue to speak their decisions out loud when they are in the THINK BOX, sharing their plans with their caddies.

When verbalizing your decisions they should be expressed as specifically and as positively as possible. The words you use must not be vague or weak. You must use strong, clear language. This is critical, both because it focuses your mind and because it holds doubt at bay. Say aloud: "I am going to hit a 6-iron and my target is the second tree from the right behind the green. The ball will fade to the pin." It is a clear, congruent, and committed decision. Notice that everything is stated positively. Never say: "I will try to . . ." or "I think this will . . ." Say it decisively and swing the club confidently. Nicklaus never stroked a putt until he had imagined the ball rolling to the hole, going into the cup, then popping out of the cup, and rolling back to where it started.

Verbalizing your intentions will help you focus on the target and will enable you to channel your energy toward the target and not down at the ground. Some players mentally paint the target red before each shot, but everyone should find some image that works for them. If you don't think you can execute the shot you have imagined, perhaps you have selected the wrong shot. One of the things we have discovered through our students is that the process of verbalizing their intentions for the shot can sometimes lead them to see that they have chosen the wrong shot or have decided on a course of action that is outside their skill set. Verbalizing the shot can actually help you reach a decision by forcing you to think about the shot. Clear decisions can only be reached by considering all the options.

Part of what you need to be deciding in verbalizing your intentions for the shot is where the most likely result is going to leave you. You must truly THINK in the THINK BOX. Given all of the variables involved (including a realistic evaluation of your skills), what is the best shot to hit? There are definitely times when discretion is the better part of valor. As we say in a later chapter: Don't try a shot you can't handle. Sometimes in the course of verbalizing your plan for the shot you will catch yourself snickering or giving some other indication that you don't really believe what you are saying. When you catch yourself doing that, rethink the shot.

When you practice verbalizing your intentions in the THINK BOX, you can keep a scorecard of how you do. Rate yourself 1 (low) to 5 (high) on how clearly you stated your intention for the shot and on how committed you remained to that decision throughout the shot. Don't worry about where the ball went or how the shot turned out. What you should be judging is how strongly you stayed focused on your intention for the shot. Remember, we can do everything right and have a bad result. That's part of what makes golf such a great game. Our focus should be on the process, not the outcome. If we take care of the process, the outcome will take care of itself. It comes down to this: *Say it! Mean it! Do it!*

The purpose of the THINK BOX/PLAY BOX is to have your mind as uncluttered as possible when you cross the DE-CISION LINE and step up to hit the ball. It should be an act as instinctual as getting onto a bicycle and pedaling off. This can be achieved by narrowing your focus as much as possible. THINK BOX: What do I want to do with this shot? I want to put it in the fairway so I can get a point. How should I get it in the fairway? The wind is blowing left to right and the fairway slopes gradually to the right. My normal ball flight is left-to-right. If I hit a driver solidly I can reach that left fairway bunker. I'm going to play a 3-wood at the left edge of that bunker and the wind, the slope, and my fade will carry the ball to the right edge of the bunker, but short of it because I hit a 3-wood. This will leave me a manageable 175 yards into the green.

The key is to determine what works for you. It is important to learn to trust your instincts. People think that decision making is merely gathering information and then making a decision. It is much more than that. A key component of the information you gather is the self-awareness to understand what will work best for you. By playing the think game you can learn more about what works best for you, and the more you know about what works for you the more committed you will be to the shot you are going to hit.

That said, there is nothing left to do but to step into the PLAY BOX and hit the shot. This all seems simplistic, and it is. **Golf is nowhere near as complicated as most people would have you believe.** When you are in the THINK BOX develop a plan of action. Stay committed to your PLAYING FOCUS, make a clear and congruent decision, and then step into the PLAY BOX with complete commitment to the shot. Remember, determining your PLAYING FOCUS should occur before the round. And remember also, your PLAYING FOCUS can change from day to day.

THINK BOX/PLAY BOX and the concept of a PLAYING FOCUS that is under your control provide a solid framework within which to build a reliable game of golf. Now let's start to sharpen some of the skills we need to function at our highest levels both in the THINK BOX and in the PLAY BOX. Some of those skills are mechanical, many of them are mental, and all of them need to act in concert with each other in order for the golf swing to function properly. A good place to start is to learn a little bit more about yourself and understand exactly how your body functions when your mind allows fear and a lack of confidence to seep into the swing.

CHAPTER VI

You Are More Consistent Than You Think

"The greatest discovery of our generation is that human beings can alter their lives by altering their attitudes of mind. As you think, so shall you be."

—WILLIAM JAMES, NINETEENTH-CENTURY AMERICAN PHILOSOPHER

SWING KEY: Expand your confidence zone by knowing your tendencies.

Before students attend our school, we ask them a series of questions. One of them is: "What do you hope to get out of your experience with GOLF54?" Among the most common answers is, "I want my play to be more consistent." Actually, we are all very consistent, just not always in the ways we would like to be. What most players are really looking for is not so much to be more consistent but rather to break the patterns in which their games get stuck. You are way more consistent than you think, and by understanding the patterns of your play you will learn to recognize your tendencies and escape them. Hitting a wild slice into the trees on a crucial hole in a match is not necessarily being inconsistent. Many times it is a very common result of how your swing betrays you under pressure.

In all areas of our personalities—remember, we are working with the whole person here, not just the golfer—there are essential characteristics that reveal themselves when we are under pressure. That is when our true self emerges. In social settings it might be nervous laughter, on the job it might be reacting defensively when something about your work is called into question, and in sports it could be a number of different ways in which tension manifests itself. What is important to understand is that there is a very consistent pattern in how your body reacts to stress. As in all areas of human development, the key to controlling or changing how we act under stress is understanding the patterns of our behavior. The key to hitting good golf shots is confidence, and the key to developing confidence is understanding how your mind and body react to pressure.

What's the difference between our good shots and our bad shots? More often than not it is simply a matter of trust. How do we develop trust? By having a routine that we believe in. Are we ever going to lose trust? Of course. It happens in all areas of our lives. The important question is this: How do we get trust back when it runs out on us? Trust doesn't really go away; it merely hides. It is always in you. It's just that sometimes something gets in the way. The first step in reclaiming trust is realizing that you are losing it. The second step is honesty. How many times have you made a shot selection based on your perfect shot, not your average shot?

Many times, after a round of golf that was unfolding in a very promising manner but then turned bad, it is not until after the round that we are able to put our finger on exactly when the wheels came off the track. Of course, it is too late then. And the futility of the situation is compounded by the fact that, while we may have identified when things started going badly, we did not identify what was going on that made the golf swing turn into a crude imitation of itself. You need to learn what you do and how you feel when you are playing well, and you need to learn what is different when things fall apart. This will help you learn what tools work best for you.

The following drill will help you identify how your body and mind react under stress. More accurately, it will show you what happens to you when you have left your confidence zone—when you have lost trust.

One of the best exercises you can do to build confidence on the golf course involves a bucket of balls that you never hit. Try this exercise: Take a handful of balls, stand over an empty bucket, and drop several balls into the bucket. It's a simple enough task. Take one step back and toss several more into the bucket. Still a piece of cake. Take another step back and do the same. Notice how your body feels. Notice your mind: Is it quiet or are you talking to yourself? How does that change as you move farther away? Do you see the target? If so, how do you see it? Do your legs tighten? Do your arms tense?

Do you see the ball flight? Keep moving back until your trust level changes. Does the ball sometimes go in but in your heart you know that it was luck? This is important to notice because it is essential not to confuse outcome with trust. What do you see, hear, feel, and think that is different when you leave your area of trust?

This drill will help you understand how your body reacts under stress. Lynn found that when she started to leave her confidence zone, her knees would lock up. This is exactly what happens to her on the golf course under pressure. Lynn's bad swings result from a restricted pivot because tension has taken over her knees. Another student noticed that, as he became less confident, he would squeeze the ball tighter. This is exactly one of his tension-induced flaws on the golf course— his grip pressure becomes too tight. Yet another student found that he rushed the throw, almost as if he were less likely to miss if he got the throwing motion over with quickly. **You can't make fear go away, but you can expand your confidence zone by knowing your tendencies when faced with fear.**

Do these mistakes sound familiar? This drill functions in the same way therapy functions. By understanding the patterns of your behavior, you come to be better able to control undesirable behavior. By understanding your tendencies better, you can develop techniques to get back to strategies you use when you have trust. When you talk to someone who has just had a round of golf get away from him, you detect two distinct patterns. One pattern is for the player to say that he had no idea how badly he was unraveling until after the round was over, when a mental reconstruction made it all painfully obvious. The second tendency is for the player to say that he could see himself losing control—almost as if he were a spectator to his own life—but was unable to step in and take control of events. In both cases, the problem is that the player was not in touch with himself enough—and with his tendencies under pressure—to step in and redirect a bad situation as it was developing.

When you feel trust slipping away on the golf course, it is essential to refocus on the positive. Remember, trust isn't gone, it is merely hiding, and you can find it again with the proper tools. This is when you must concentrate on getting back your trust or "go" signals. Lynn needs to get her "Tigger knees" back and unlock her legs. Pia needs to silence the internal "chatter" that clogs up her head. And Annika needs to slow things down. By understanding your tendencies, you can develop trust in your game by pushing fear back into the corner where it belongs. Perhaps most importantly, by gaining a greater knowledge of how you react under stress, you can learn how to reclaim trust in your swing and in your decision making when trust seems to be running out on you on the golf course. As you become better at recognizing when you are leaving your confidence zone, you will become better at reclaiming it. You will learn to focus on what you want to get back to and how you want to get there. Maybe it is as simple as walking more slowly or taking deep breaths. Maybe you just need to ask yourself, "How am I when I play good golf?"

Everyone who has played the game of golf long enough has a memory bank of bad shots that tend to creep out at the worst possible times. Perhaps you are playing very well and then you hit a poor shot and that voice in your head says, "Here it comes. It is all going to unravel now." The first crucial step is to be honest enough and understand yourself well enough to recognize that negative thought when it surfaces in your brain. The second step is to ask this crucial question: "Is that true?" The answer—always—is "No." It can't be true because it hasn't happened yet. This is a crucial point in a round of golf. This is when you need to recommit to THINK BOX/PLAY BOX and to your PLAYING FOCUS. Just because something bad has happened in the past does not mean it has to happen again in the future. **You can't alter what has happened, but you can influence what will happen.**

One obstacle we all must overcome is that it is easier to remember our bad shots than it is to remember our good ones. Strangely, we all seem to have a tendency to not put enough value on what we do right, almost as if we view our successes as accidents instead of as the result of our well-planned actions. It is almost as if we fall into the trap of thinking that we do not deserve success. One way to expand your confidence zone is to highlight in bright pink what it is that you do right. Keep a journal. Write down the good shots you hit. Embed them in your memory bank so you can draw on those positive memories later when you need them on the golf course.

Tossing golf balls into a bucket probably seems like a waste of practice time, but try it. Once you discipline your mind to be in tune to what is happening to your body as it leaves its confidence zone, you will understand more clearly the way the entire you, the whole you, reacts to pressure. As with everything else we do, the first step to changing undesirable behavior is to recognize it. The second step is to understand that behavior so that we can reach the crucial third step: changing it. The golf ball–tossing drill may seem like a simplistic activity, but if you are paying attention, if you are listening to your body, you can gain a greater understanding of how you react to stress. That is an insight that can be beneficial on and off the golf course.

The golf ball–tossing drill can also be beneficial in two other ways. Some players use it as part of their pre-round routine as a way to help focus their thoughts. You can't get the ball in the bucket unless you concentrate on the bucket in a way that a warm-up on the range doesn't always focus concentration. It can be almost like a meditation before a round of golf. On the range you focus your swing for the competition ahead. With the ball–tossing drill, you can focus the mind for the concentration needed to compete successfully. This drill can help you warm up your confidence before a round, and it can serve as a quick-fix trust cure during a round.

Once the round has started, the simple act of tossing a golf ball can be a useful drill that can help relieve stress and refocus concentration when the tension of the moment has the mind scurrying in a million different directions. As you are standing on the tee box, waiting to hit a shot, take a ball and toss it in the air a foot or so and catch it. Not only will the repetitive motion relax you, but once again concentrating on catching the ball will force your mind to refocus on the task at hand—to focus on the now. It will get you out of future think or stop you from dwelling on a past failure by bringing your mind back to the now. In this instant, the task is catching the ball. When you stick the tee in the ground, the task on which you will be focusing will be hitting the next shot.

Once again, an act as simple as tossing a ball into a bucket or tossing a ball up into the air and catching it can serve a complex array of purposes. The bucket drill will help you understand how your body reacts under pressure. The drill in which you toss a ball into the air and catch it will help you bring your body and your mind back under control when it is feeling the increased pressure of a competitive round. Remember, the key to handling pressure and deflecting tension is not to deny their existence, but rather to acknowledge that they are there and neutralize them by embracing them.

CHAPTER VII

Anger Makes Us Stupid

"The two qualities that helped most: honesty about my game, and a sense of humor."
—JOYCE WETHERED, WINNER OF FIVE CONSECUTIVE ENGLISH WOMEN'S AMATEUR CHAMPIONSHIPS IN THE 1920S

SWING KEY: Find something good to say about every shot you hit—or say nothing.

The stories are in the newspapers every day and on the TV news virtually each night. Maybe they involve road rage. Maybe they involve an incident of domestic violence. Maybe they involve an argument over something as seemingly inconsequential as an accidentally rude encounter between two people on a crowded bus. Whatever the case, the pattern is the same: Someone gets angry and does something stupid. After the fact it seems so obvious what happened. But after the fact is exactly that. The key to stopping these emotionally triggered catastrophes is to recognize them as they are developing.

In golf, a round can unravel in much the way a sweater falls apart when curious fingers pick at a single thread, impulsively tugging at it until a loose fraction of an inch becomes an ever-growing length expanding with alarming speed. Oftentimes the catalyst for the destruction of a round of golf is not so much a poorly hit shot as it is the reaction to that shot. Bad shots are going to happen. Anyone who has played the game knows that. The key to success is not in eliminating our mistakes—mistakes are going to happen for everyone—but in controlling our reactions to those mistakes. One of the most overlooked parts of golf is the post-shot routine. It is there that you build memory that will affect future shots.

The most destructive force you can unleash on the golf course is anger. **An impulsive reaction against a perceived injustice is never prudent behavior.** A bad swing can make us feel stupid, and a bad bounce can make us feel unlucky, but the worst reaction to misfortune is anger. That reaction all but guarantees that more poor shots are to come. Poor decision making is one way anger manifests itself. We knew a player who got so anxious that in a tournament, when he intended to hit a 6-iron he grabbed a 9-iron instead, leaving the shot well short in the middle of a pond. Simply put, anger makes us stupid. It clouds our judgment and makes us more likely to react with only our lower brain functions. Anger denies us access to our higher brain functions and reduces us to operating from the reptilian and mammalian brain.

Anger not only triggers hormones that create tension and anxiety in the body, but those hormones then shut down parts of the brain and lead us to make bad decisions. How many times have you hit your tee shot into the trees and then, in a fit of anger, tried to do too much with your second shot and ended up making a triple bogey? The disappointment with the drive leads you to attempt to erase the poor shot with one swing. And we all know how that works out. More often than not, a gamble is greeted with a ball clunking off a tree or remaining in the rough.

The frustrating thing is that on many of those occasions, when you looked back at the round you wondered why you didn't just pitch back to the fairway and settle for a bogey—or maybe make a one-putt par. Anger opens the door to a variety of mistakes: bad decisions, hesitant swings, rushed tempo, and even not seeing the line to the target clearly.

Dealing with anger is not an easy thing, but anger can be controllable with the proper recognition of what is going on around you. Few players have controlled their emotions on the golf course as well as Jack Nicklaus. Lynn, who worked for the Nicklaus Company for five years, remembers one time at the Doral tournament when Jack's tee shot on the eighteenth hole ended up in a divot. How did Nicklaus react? "I thought, 'It will help me stay down better,'" Jack recounted later. Instead of reacting poorly, Nicklaus turned a negative into a positive. That is pure control on the course.

All golf instructors talk a lot about pre-shot routine, but you rarely hear them discuss post-shot routine when, in fact, it is a key component to emotional management on the golf course. How you choose to react emotionally in the finish position of your swing will highly influence your future game. Your brain will record that reaction, and that memory will trigger the release of chemicals that can have either a positive or a negative effect on your body and on how you function both mentally and physically. When you have a similar shot in the future, the memory filed away by your emotional reaction in the past will trigger a physiological stress reaction that might lead to the same result. You can insure better shots in the future with a more positive post-shot routine now.

Emotions have a tendency to snowball, or spiral, either in a positive or negative direction. A positive, UPWARD SPIRAL is the ideal emotional state on the golf course. Here's how it works: When teeing off on the first hole, try to start out emotionally neutral. After a couple of good shots, you become more interested in what you're doing—you're there, in the present, and can't wait to hit the next shot. This makes you play even better. Now you're starting to get engaged. You don't just make clear decisions; you have the courage to go through with them. After a few holes like this, you start feeling confident and saying good things to yourself such as, "I know I can do this" and, "I trust myself with this shot."

Once this level has been reached, you're likely to slip into that elusive zone we all try so hard to find. This is where everything just flows; your mind and body work effortlessly together, and everything clicks with remarkable ease. The final upward spiral stage is pure euphoria. You feel total happiness and well-being, and your internal "pharmacy" is flooding your system with healthy chemicals. We have a former student who went from a 7 handicap to a 1 handicap mostly by focusing on his post-shot routine and by learning how to associate with his good shots and dissociate from his bad ones. And his friends also tell us he has become more fun to play with because he no longer has extreme mood swings.

Unfortunately, many golfers end up sliding into the opposite, DOWNWARD SPIRAL instead. After hitting a shot that isn't 100 percent right, you might feel a slight hesitation when standing over the ball. This likely makes you hit another mediocre shot. Your mind starts spinning with questions: "Is my ball position correct?" "What was that I heard on *Academy Live*?" Now you're confused. On the next few shots you try a slew of different swing thoughts but nothing works, making you frustrated—"I knew this was going to happen!" You quickly turn from frustration to anger and even start cursing or calling yourself names. After anger always comes depression, and by then you might as well add ten shots to your score. To have a chance of getting yourself started on an upward spiral, you must abort the downward spiral before you reach frustration. How? **Learn to ASSOCIATE and DISSOCIATE.**

To experience something emotionally is to be ASSOCIATED; to do so without emotional involvement means that you are DISSOCIATED. If you can teach yourself to associate with the good things and dissociate from the bad, your game will improve dramatically over time.

TO ASSOCIATE:

- Come up with a joyous hand or body gesture (like Tiger's pumped fist), which you repeat after every good shot. This will help you imprint the memory of the good shot in your brain and make it a positive part of your golf history.

- Let the wonderful feeling you experience after a good shot spread through your body; truly experience it before moving on to the next shot. Soak in the moment. Enjoy your success. We always hear professional players talking about "learning how to win." A big part of that is accumulating positive memories to draw upon in the future.

- When you hit a poor shot, immediately replay it in your mind—not as a miss, but with the originally desired outcome. Make your memory of the shot be as you intended it to be, not as it turned out.

TO DISSOCIATE:

- After a bad shot, take a deep breath, step to the side, and observe yourself as if you are on the outside looking in. Imagine a television screen around what just happened. You can see and hear the bad experience, but you're not emotionally attached to it. To react with anger will only imprint a negative feeling in your golf memory that will haunt you later.

- React to your own miss as you would if someone else hit a bad shot. Follow the ball with your eyes and stay focused on where it's going. Since, in your mind, it's not your ball,

you can keep your emotions out of it. Make it all something you saw, not something you did. At the Broadmoor
in 1995, when Annika won the U.S. Women's Open for
the first time, she drove into the rough on the seventeenth
hole. She had never won an LPGA event before and there
was a lot of pressure on her. In her shot out of the rough
her iron caught in the high grass and she hit a duck hook.
Her reaction? She turned around and started to laugh. That
was something she was taught. The memory of that shot
was not filed away.

The ability to associate and dissociate will fill your inner
emotional memory bank with positive, uplifting feelings and
keep the negative, destructive ones at bay. We often say that to
learn to associate and dissociate is the fundamental basis of
confidence in the long term. You have fundamentals with the
swing, and you should have them for your confidence. Take
care of it!

To dissociate is not about denial but rather about objective
learning. Get the learning but not the storage. Storage is the
root of the "yips." When you file away bad memories it leads
to bad behavior in the future, and on the golf course that
translates into bad shots. And remember: This doesn't just apply to the golf course—it's a great way of enhancing everyday
life as well. Hold on to the positive and let go of the negative.
**Find something good to say about every shot you
hit—or say nothing.**

Try the following drills to help control your emotions:

- Practice dissociation by playing nine holes without making any judgments, good or bad, on any part of your game or your partners' games. Grumpy or giddy body language or facial expressions and words like "bad" and "good" are taboo. What does this feel like to you? What's easy and what's hard about it? Playing "no-judgment golf" is the first step to recognizing that you are able to control your emotions and always return to neutral. This is the key to getting the wheels back on track when they come off, one of the aspects of the game with which players struggle most.

- Another drill with which to learn a positive post-shot routine is to play nine holes and after each shot, no matter what happens and even if the ball leaves the property, you remain either neutral or happy. That's what you want to learn to do all the time in both practice and play. Stay neutral or without judgment to the shots you don't like and take in some degree of happiness for your good shots.

  Give yourself a score on the 1 to 5 scale after each shot, measuring how successfully you stayed positive or neutral. Remember, you are not measuring the outcome of the shot, just your reaction to it.

- Allow yourself a limited time after your shot is completed to make derogatory comments about the outcome. Ask your partner to signal you when the time is up, at which point you must let go of the past and refocus on the next shot. Earl Woods, Tiger's father, developed a similar system for his son when he was a teenager, giving him ten seconds in which to be disappointed with a shot before he had to move on. That's a good first step, but learning to associate and dissociate right away is the ultimate in the post-shot routine.

We tend to think of the way we react emotionally to situations as merely being "the way we are," but the truth is, our reactions are controllable. Think of the last bad decision you made on the golf course. Did mismanaged emotions play a part in that decision? Did you overreact and make that decision based on a knee-jerk reaction after a previously missed shot?

Current research clearly indicates that performance is directly influenced by stress and emotional mismanagement. The Institute of HeartMath®, a world leader in human performance research, has validated that emotional reactiveness and stress, which we often experience as inner turmoil, can inhibit the cortical regions of the brain. With the cortical functions inhibited, problem-solving is hampered, reaction speeds and coordination are impaired, and we cannot think as clearly. Decisions are less effective, our listening skills are impaired, and creativity is obstructed. It's literally true that anger makes us stupid!

Researcher and author Joseph Chilton Pearce says that when we become upset for any reason, "all neural action, learning, memory, cognition, problem-solving, and so on are adversely affected." Our emotional state is critical to what we learn and how well we can recall and apply what we have learned. Built into the emotional-cognitive structures of the brain are many evolutionary functions that date back to our species' struggle for survival and the mechanisms that evolved to cope with stress.

Structures like the amygdala in the "emotional," or limbic, region of the brain can "hijack" the intellectual process when intense emotions are experienced. This is why even very smart people can make foolish choices under stress.

So how does this relate to your golf? Every time you hit a golf shot something happens. The ball starts at one point and travels to another point. Now what takes place almost instantaneously in the brain is some judgment of that reality. You either like where the ball went or you don't. Based on those emotions and the resulting chemical flush you experience, you either move your system toward a state of coherence—where the heart and brain work together—or away from it.

We have all experienced moments of coherence when things seemed in sync. We were in "flow," our ACTIONS and INTENTIONS matched, and the OUTCOME was PRODUCTIVE, efficient, and fulfilling. Coherence is the underlying principle of what makes a laser so powerful. A laser produces coherent light waves that are highly efficient. The shift from incoherence to coherence can bring dramatic effects: a sixty-watt lightbulb whose light waves could be made as coherent as a laser would have the power to bore a hole through the sun from ninety million miles away!

This same analogy can be applied to understanding human performance. Psychophysiological coherence, as scientists at HeartMath have labeled it, is a highly ordered state where emotions, mind, and body are operating with a greater degree of harmony. It's exciting to know that this internal coherence can actually be measured by monitoring the synchronization of the autonomic nervous system, brain, and heart. HeartMath's research shows us that you can determine whether the nervous system is full of noise or static-free. As HeartMath's founder, Doc Childre, says, **"Coherence is efficiency in action."** Attention span, mental clarity, and creativity naturally increase. Power is maximized. Coherent human beings, including golfers, thrive mentally, emotionally, and physically.

So the bottom line is that your emotional reaction after the shot determines whether you are going to build up your reserves of coherence or deplete them. Your emotional judgment or reaction is a choice in how you want to perceive reality. How do you determine that choice? Go back to when the ball left the clubface and began its journey. This is the precise moment of emotional management. Stop any reaction you might have *immediately*. Don't get caught up in where the ball is going and what it means to you. Just begin counting *slowly* to seven. One one thousand, two one thousand, and so on.

In those seven seconds, you can stop the emotional hijacking (the amygdala looking for an emotional match to a previous experience) and become neutral to the event. You have created a space where you can consciously make a choice of perception. You are aware. You are in control of your emotions. Now create the emotion or judgment that best serves your future for the next shot, the rest of the round, or your golfing career. Learn to react in a neutral or happy way. We believe that those seven seconds are one key to reaching your greatest potential—your 54.

CHAPTER VIII

Don't Play the Blame Game

"Always bear in mind that your own resolution to succeed is more important than any other one thing."
—ABRAHAM LINCOLN, U.S. PRESIDENT, 1861–65

SWING KEY: Accept responsibility. The only one who can rescue you is you.

Almost everyone who has played the game of golf has seen the movie *Caddyshack* and laughed as the Chevy Chase character describes his PLAYING FOCUS as "See the ball, be the ball." In fact, that goofy character is doing several things right in determining his PLAYING FOCUS: He is stating it positively, he is stating it specifically, and it is a goal that is under his control. When the Chase character holes a putt while blindfolded, we laugh, but the truth of the matter is that he has succeeded because he has surrendered himself to total trust. The first step to hitting a good golf shot is a belief that you can hit a good golf shot. The second step—just as important—is to accept responsibility when things do not go as planned. It is when faced with adversity that you must truly "see the ball, be the ball."

As we said earlier, one of the key components of success in golf is a belief that you have properly prepared yourself to play. A second essential element is the full commitment to and trust in the shot you are about to hit. Again, crucial to changing destructive behavior is recognizing it and altering it before it takes on a life of its own. Earlier we talked about recognizing what you can and cannot control on the golf course. Now let's talk about what you can and cannot control in your behavior on the golf course.

A common challenge for golfers of all skill levels is to avoid turning on themselves when things start to go poorly. The least painful way to turn on yourself is not to attack yourself but to sabotage your game by placing blame everywhere except where it belongs—which is likely your own loss of focus. We call this self-destructive state the VERBs. In short, your reaction to a series of bad shots is to lash out at the world around you rather than accepting responsibility for your actions. The result is less focus. You are playing the blame game rather than playing the game of golf—all but insuring more bad shots. We were inspired in this line of thinking by the book *What Happy People Know* by Dan Baker.

VERBs is a self-pitying state where you see yourself as the

VICTIM who is ENTITLED to better and instead of working wants to be RESCUED from a fate that you BLAME on
conditions outside yourself. Does this sound familiar? It is a
style of behavior that is in no way unique to golf. We don't
get the job we want and we blame the boss for poor judgment. It rains on your vacation and you see it as another way
in which you are victimized. You play the lottery hoping to
be rescued from your dead-end job rather than working to
find another.

The golf course is an easy place to fall into this kind of behavior. You hit a couple of bad shots or you get a couple of
bad bounces and you start to blame everyone and everything
except yourself. Anyone who was paying close attention early
in the week at the 2004 Ryder Cup at Oakland Hills near De-
troit would not have been too surprised that the European
team gave the U.S. team its worst defeat in the seventy-seven-
year history of the event. The American team was completely
locked into a VERB mentality. Let's take a look.

VICTIMS

The U.S. players said over and over again that they were in a
no-win situation. Because they were expected to triumph, the
excuse went, they would not get adequate praise if they pulled
off the victory and would be soundly criticized if they lost.
Instead of walking in with their heads high, focused only on
victory, they arrived at Oakland Hills already armed with an
excuse, thus establishing the foundation for a self-fulfilling
prophecy.

ENTITLED

One of the constant complaints of the American team was the number of social events they had to attend in the days before the competition started. In addition to the opening ceremony and media obligations, there were several cocktail parties and dinners held to please the major financial supporters of the Ryder Cup. Many players on the U.S. team complained early in the week that it was difficult to get ready for competition when they had to meet those evening obligations. To try to take some strain off his players, U.S. team captain Hal Sutton told his players not to sign autographs during practice rounds. Meanwhile, European captain Bernhard Langer told his players to sign autographs, which helped ease animosity the home fans might have had for the visiting team and helped Langer's team relax and have fun. The European team viewed the social obligations as part of the process—and fun—not as drudgery or obstacles to success.

RESCUED

Another common refrain from the American players was that they never play well in better-ball and alternate-shot competition, but that the true cream would rise to the top on Sunday in singles play. Unfortunately, while the Americans were waiting to be rescued by singles play, the Europeans were building such a large lead that the chance of a comeback was all but erased before play started on Sunday.

BLAME

As soon as the competition was over, the Americans began blaming everyone except themselves. They blamed the media, saying that by making the U.S. team heavy favorites the press had convinced the public that the European team was not as strong as it really was. They blamed the Official World Ranking, saying that the reason more Americans were highly ranked was because of a flaw in the system that gave more points to PGA Tour events than to European Tour events. And they blamed the fact that the Americans have a team-style event every year—either the Ryder Cup or the Presidents Cup—while the Europeans only have to face that pressure every other year.

It could very well be that a major reason the European teams have taken home the Ryder Cup in seven of the last ten competitions is that they enter the event with an entirely different attitude. It seems as if the Europeans come into the Ryder Cup with two goals: have fun and win. It seems as if they understand that if they have fun, the winning will most likely take care of itself. The Americans more and more appear to view the Ryder Cup as a chore while the Europeans see it as a challenge to relish. That positive feeling that they bring into the competition has translated into success. The VERB attitude of the Americans has translated into disaster. **They refused to accept responsibility and never grasped that the only one who can rescue you is you.**

On the flip side of things, the U.S. Ryder Cup team at Brookline in 1999 was able to use adversity to create the positive emotional energy that enabled them to stage the greatest comeback in the history of the event. The Americans went out Sunday and won the first seven singles events, and it was clear from watching U.S. players that they were functioning on a rare and wonderful plane. They were in a coherent state in which the heart and brain were acting as one. The usually stoic David Duval reacted by running in circles slapping high fives with fans after he won his match. We all know the reaction on the seventeenth green when Justin Leonard holed a crucial forty-foot putt in his match against Jose Maria Olazabal and dozens of Americans, overcome by joy, ran onto the green. Somehow on Saturday night, that team pulled together and turned adversity into a rallying point for greatness. The lesson is this: How you react is a choice you have, and it is a crucial choice.

When you feel yourself on the edge of VERBs, there are two essential questions you need to ask yourself:

1. Is that true?
2. What can I do about it?

These simple questions can help put doubt into perspective. Again, Annika uses the tools of GOLF54 better than anyone. When a negative thought enters her mind she is brilliant at asking herself, "Is that true?" The answer to that question— if it involves doubt or a negative memory—is usually "no" since the event in question (your next shot) hasn't happened yet. We have actually seen Annika say at a tournament, "I'm whining," and then stop!

At the 2000 U.S. Women's Open near Chicago, we were with Annika on the range and she started complaining about the practice facility. "It's downhill," she said. "It's downwind and I can't get a sense of how my shots are going." Pia let Annika get it all off her chest and then asked: "Annika, what can you do about it?" Annika answered: "You always ask me those questions." Then she thought for a moment, talked with her caddie, and they were the only two who took some balls and went to the back of the range and hit backward. She diffused a negative by developing a plan of action rather than merely complaining about it.

Part of the discipline professional golfers need to develop is to not let the distractions they face during a round shake their mental clarity. Many times a pro will walk up to his ball only to hear a marshal say, "Boy, you got a bad lie," or, "No one has made a putt from there all day." At times like these it is essential to ask the questions:

Is that true?
What am I going to do about it?

There are many ways these questions can benefit the recreational golfer as well. Say you are playing an important match at your club and you awake to find a light rain falling. The first thought that enters your head is: "I am a terrible rain player. I have no chance today." So you ask: "Is that true?" The answer is: "I may have struggled in the rain in the past but that does not mean that that is the case today. This is a new round over which I have control." Then you ask: "What am I going to do about it?" One option could be to say to yourself: "I will use the rain to focus more on a slow takeaway and better balance. After each shot I will hold my follow-through for a three-count to insure that I am not rushing things." You can also focus on the aspects of the rain you can control, like keeping your clubs dry, wearing proper rain gear, and deciding whether gloves work for you. And remember: It is raining for your opponent also.

Here is a drill that can help you learn to store the kind of positive memories and emotional energy that will make both your brain and your body perform at peak levels.

In this exercise you will give yourself a grade after each shot on a 1 to 5 scale, with 5 being the highest mark. Again, this drill is best done if you can play with a partner, but it is also possible to do it alone. Here is what we want you to do. Get into the THINK BOX and verbalize your intentions for the shot you are about to hit. Then step into the PLAY BOX and execute the shot. After each shot, grade yourself on three things:

How committed were you to the shot? Did you make a firm decision about the shot you were about to play? As you stepped into the PLAY BOX did you have any doubt about your shot selection? Grade your mental preparation for the shot on a 1 to 5 scale with 1 being the lowest and 5 being the highest. Did you feel you committed fully to the shot? Score yourself honestly.

How well did you execute the shot? This is an evaluation of your performance in the PLAY BOX. How successfully did you carry out the mission you had mapped out in the THINK BOX? A shot can fail for several reasons. One could be a bad plan; a second could be a lack of full commitment to the plan; and a third can be poor physical execution of the plan. Again, grade your physical execution of the plan on a 1-to-5 scale. And remember, just because the ball ended up on the bunker does not necessarily mean that you executed the shot poorly. Don't confuse execution with outcome.

How successfully did you keep your attitude positive or neutral (not negative) after the shot? The surest way to guarantee that the next shot you hit will be a poor one is to not let go of the shot you have just hit. Anger over a poor shot, as we have already discussed, can lead to poor decision making and poor execution of future shots. After you struck the ball did you maintain a positive or neutral attitude, no matter the result of the shot? Again, grade yourself on a 1-to-5 scale.

As we did with the point game, at the end of the round use these scores to evaluate your play, not your actual score. Remember, score is not a controllable goal, but PREPARATION, EXECUTION, and REACTION are controllable goals.

One of the great things about golf is that every shot we have is the absolute only time we are ever going to hit that shot. This exercise will help you learn to treat every shot with the respect that it deserves. And this exercise will help you channel your focus away from the uncontrollable and back to the controllable, where it belongs. This exercise will help you be the ball. And it will help you create a nonVERBal culture.

CHAPTER IX

Let the Target Be Your Guide

"Self-trust is the first secret of success."
—RALPH WALDO EMERSON, NINETEENTH-CENTURY
AMERICAN AUTHOR

SWING KEY: Channel your energy toward the target
and the ball will follow.

There may be no area of life in which the phenomenon of the self-fulfilling prophecy is more common than golf. How many times have you switched to an old ball before you teed off over a water hazard and then hit the ball in the drink? How many times have you stepped onto a tee box and said, "I never play this hole well," and then made a triple bogey? How many times have you picked a bunker as a target, figuring your normal fade would carry the ball back to the fairway, only to hit one of your rare straight balls right into the sand? One of the best ways to stay out of trouble is to not allow trouble into the equation. Don't allow yourself to think about hitting it into the water, and don't use a hazard as a directional line. It will become a magnet that draws in your ball.

We had a student recently who, in one of our classroom rounds, stepped up onto the first tee with two golf balls, tossing one to the side of the tee marker while he teed up the other one. When asked what he was doing, he said he was being prepared in case he had to hit a second ball. What he was really doing was setting the stage for failure. There is a big difference between playing a smart shot and playing a defensive shot. One of the most thoughtful players ever in the professional game was Nick Faldo, the six-time major championship winner. He once said, "Golf is not about the quality of your good shots, it is about the quality of your bad shots." What he was saying is that score is more affected by the penalties for poor play than by the rewards for good play. That's an important thing to remember.

The connection between the mind and the body on the golf course cannot be overestimated. They can work together in a harmonious way or they can function at cross-purposes. And one way to virtually guarantee that the mind sabotages the body is to allow negative thoughts to control your decision making. Again, this becomes a matter of the self-fulfilling prophecy. Combating it becomes a matter of listening to your body closely enough to understand when doubt is creeping into the shot-selection process. Walking onto the tee box with a second ball to hit is only one of many ways we sabotage the swing.

How many times has this happened to you? Your normal shot shape is a controlled fade. You hit a good drive and arrive at the ball to find that the next shot requires a 5-iron to a green guarded by water on the right side. Instead of playing your normal shot—aiming at the left edge of the green and trusting that your normal fade will carry the ball back to the pin—you protect against the hazard on the right side and aim farther to left. But what often happens is that, in the PLAY BOX, you lose confidence in the decision you have made and aim even farther left—at least that's what you think you are doing. What you are really doing is opening your stance and your shoulders, guaranteeing an outside-in swing even more pronounced than usual, resulting not in a controlled fade but rather in a wild slice or a huge pull, sending the ball into the very hazard you thought you were avoiding or deep into the rough on the other side of the fairway.

What happened here? It was simply a matter of a loss of trust. It was also probably a matter of breaking from routine. A lot of times, when we step up to a shot in a pressure situation like this, we make subtle changes after we have addressed the ball. You look at the target and—aware of the hazard on the right—lose confidence in the shot you have selected. Your mind tells your body to compensate by borrowing more from the left side of the fairway. But instead of stepping away from the ball and realigning with a target farther left, you move your feet and shoulders farther to the left. This opens the stance and throws the swing plane even more outside the intended line of flight than usual. You made a THINK BOX decision in the PLAY BOX. Result: a wild slice or a huge pull.

If you step to the shot and suddenly lose confidence in the shot you have selected, step away from the ball and draw up a new plan. If you decide that the prudent miss is in the left rough or the left bunker, refocus with that as your target. The key is that your mind is focused ON WHERE YOU WANT TO HIT THE BALL AND NOT WHERE YOU DON'T WANT TO HIT THE BALL. It is extremely difficult to make a good golf swing if you are making it with a sense of fear. There is a huge difference between good course management and playing afraid. **The fearful swing rarely produces a courageous shot. If you channel your energy toward the target, the ball will follow.**

In discussing the difficulty of putting the steeply contoured, extremely fast greens at Augusta National Golf Club, Colin Montgomerie once said: "As soon as you start worrying about the putt you are going to have coming back, you have missed the putt you have." That is a very wise observation. While golf is like billiards in that you want to play this shot with the idea of setting up the next shot, the shot you are hitting can only be properly executed through total commitment. Fear enters the picture when you lose confidence in your preparation. The pros call that sort of defensive swing a "steer job."

One of the drills we do in our school to build total commitment to the shot is a chipping drill. We have a player stand at address with six balls near the practice green and have them pick a target to chip to. They pick a line, decide on a target, and make a decision about how hard to hit the shot in the think box. When they step into the play box we tell them that instead of looking to the ball, they should look to the target. Then we have them chip. We find that our students are startled by two things: first, by the fact that they make such good contact with the ball, and second, by the result. This drill is also a very effective way to practice putting.

What happens in this drill is the player is learning to release his or her energy outward and toward the target and not downward and toward the ground. Players have been told over and over again the importance of keeping their head down, so that they tend to overreact and focus so hard on keeping their head down that they don't release toward the target. Again, it is a matter of trust. Your eye was on the ball at the moment of contact, but striking the ball is only one part of the equation. The target is the other crucial component.

What this drill teaches us is that the ball, clubhead, and hands all need to follow the same path down the target line. All of your energy must be released directly at the target. Frequently, when there is trouble to the right of the target, for example, we try to steer the ball away from the hazard by making an exaggerated motion to the left. This only compounds the problem by creating a more outside-in swing and putting more slice spin on the ball. It insures the self-fulfilling prophecy. The only way to get the ball to follow the target line you have chosen is to commit totally to that target line.

Another drill that teaches you to release toward the target involves tossing a ball. The hand-pass through the hitting area in golf is a motion similar to the semi-underhand toss a baseball shortstop makes in throwing the ball to the second baseman. Take a golf ball, and with your right hand (if you are right-handed), make a motion like you are hitting a golf shot. When your hand gets to the hitting area, let go of the ball and toss it along the intended line of flight of the golf shot. You may find that your initial throws are to the left. You are holding on too long and not releasing, not totally committing to the shot. Practice this movement over and over until it becomes second nature to release and throw the golf ball at the target.

One of the things these drills teach is the discipline to commit totally to the shot. Part of what has happened to golfers is that we have become addicted to thinking. We think we have to think about the swing to make it happen. But say you are going to toss a ball. What happens? Your mind picks a target, you decide how hard to throw, and then envision the flight of the ball. Then you throw it. You do not think about the motion of throwing or the mechanics of the operation. Major league players who have gotten to where they over-think the process develop the throwing yips, sometimes to career-ending proportions, just as professional golfers have experienced career-ending putting yips. If you are going to toss a crumpled-up piece of paper into the wastebasket do you think about it—or do you just do it?

The golf swing can be as instinctual as throwing a ball. In fact, it *is* as instinctual as throwing a ball. That's why children can pick it up so easily—until adults interfere and start telling them how to do it. Push aside the mental clutter and swing.

Sometimes we concentrate so hard on some old-line thinking—like keeping our heads still and remaining behind the ball after impact—that we disrupt the natural flow of the swing toward the object of our desire—the target. Notice how totally Annika commits to the target, almost to the point where it looks like she is looking up on every shot. Her head follows her hands and the clubhead right toward the target. Don't be so focused on keeping your head down. Allow your energy to release toward the target.

When you practice hitting golf shots, bring the same mental image to the process that you would have if you were tossing a club or a ball. Pick a target—remember, in practice as in play you MUST ALWAYS HAVE A TARGET—and hit at the target with full concentration on releasing the hands at the target. In fact, pick five targets and change which one you use with each shot. This will discipline your mind to trust your swing. In the next chapter, we will learn how to build that discipline by practicing with a purpose.

CHAPTER X

Make Practice Real:
Practice with a Purpose

"For practice to have full value, make each swing
with the care of a stroke from a tee on medal day."
—JAMES BRAID, FIVE-TIME BRITISH OPEN CHAMPION
BETWEEN 1901 AND 1910

SWING KEY: Great play begins with thoughtful practice.

Practice, they say, makes perfect. But it can also be a perfectly wasteful use of time if not approached in the proper manner. In fact, time spent on the practice range can actually do more harm than good if you spend all your time perfecting bad habits—both mentally and physically. How many times do you see someone at the range who does what we call scrape-and-hit, where they just keep raking balls in front of them and banging away, with no purpose to the shot? For most people, practice ends when either the balls run out, their hands hurt, or it gets dark. But what has been accomplished? What was the purpose?

The net result of this sort of practice can be to develop—and then reinforce—sloppy habits both with the swing and with the mind. If there is not a purpose to each shot, all you are doing is encouraging the development of a loose swing. If there is not a purpose to each shot, all you are doing is teaching your mind to wander and not focus on the task at hand. How can you expect your mind and body to work together on the golf course under the pressure of a competitive round when all your practice is designed to make both your swing and your thought process lazy? The pursuit of perfection on the golf course begins on the practice range.

This may seem like stating the obvious, but if you give an honest assessment to the way you practice and if you observe the ways others practice, there will be a ring of truth to what we say here: **HAVE A PLAN when you go to the range. And MERELY HITTING BALLS for an hour is NOT A PLAN.** We once heard a non-golfer watching players warm up on the range say, "Why are they practicing missing?" Sometimes we need to change our routines to evaluate how we are playing. Here are some key exercises to help you develop a practice routine that will not only give greater focus to both your swing and your thinking, but will also release your instinctual self and give you the confidence to take that person out onto the golf course with you.

CHANGE YOUR TARGET WITH EACH SHOT.

Our entire approach to practice is that it should resemble real golf as closely as possible. It's like learning to drive a car. You can get some of the most basic stuff under control driving around in a totally empty parking lot, but does that really prepare you for driving in traffic or on an expressway at rush hour? There is no substitute for experience. Our greatest learning experiences in golf will always come on the course. The tension of hitting a golf shot that matters—whether in a tournament, playing a $2 Nassau, or trying to close out your best round ever—is unlike anything you feel on the practice range. But you can make your practice more closely resemble real golf, and thus help your game more.

The scrape-and-hit method of practice fails to simulate the most basic thing that happens on the golf course—each shot is a new experience. One thing we tend to do on the practice range is give ourselves a perfect lie for each shot. We call those "princess lies." Is that the way it happens on the golf course? It is essential to make your brain recalibrate for every shot. That is what happens on the golf course. Each shot you hit requires an entirely new thought process. What is my target? What factors (wind, lie, and so on) need I consider? How hard must I hit the shot? Do I want to play a high shot or a low one? What will the ball do after it lands? Kick to the left or right? Release and run a long way or make a pitch mark and check up?

By changing your target after each shot on the practice range, you are disciplining your mind to THINK ABOUT EACH SHOT. By taking the time to step away from each shot on the range before you hit it, you are teaching your body to HAVE A SENSE OF PURPOSE WITH EACH SWING. Hitting fifty drivers in thirty minutes does not necessarily accomplish anything. In fact, it could groove swing flaws. It is better to hit fewer shots and give them more thought. Truly, practice is a matter of quality and not quantity. If you are striving for your own 54, you want to have quality with quantity. How long can you practice and still maintain good quality?

As a discipline, go to the range and hit only ten shots in thirty minutes. This will tell you more about your skill level than almost anything else you do. Think about each shot. How many did you hit the way you planned to? Even if you are in the middle of swing changes, take breaks and simulate real golf—if you want to become a better player of the game. **You first create your habits and then your habits become you. Control what your habits become.**

CHANGE YOUR CLUB AFTER EACH SHOT.

Again, this is all about teaching your brain to recalibrate for each shot. You rarely hit consecutive drivers on the golf course—or two 6-irons in a row—unless something has gone wrong. Hit a driver on the range at a specific target. Then play a 6-iron to a different target. Follow that with a half-wedge to yet another target. Maybe play a bump-and-run with a 7-iron to a target. Then go back to the driver. If the putting green is nearby, go there also. Play every shot as a new adventure.

An excellent way to warm up for a round is to play the

golf course on the practice range. If the first hole is going to be a driver and a 4-iron for you, hit your driver and then your 4-iron. If the second hole is a par-3 where you will hit a 6-iron, play that shot, and so on until you have played all eighteen holes. This can be a useful practice routine even if you are not going to play that day. Play the course on the range anyway or, to add more fun to your practice session, play Augusta National or Pebble Beach, hitting the shots you think you would have to hit. You can also practice with a friend and play a match on the range. This could make practice not only more enjoyable but also more useful. You will be developing more discipline for both your swing and your mind.

PUTT WITH ONE BALL TO SEVERAL HOLES INSTEAD OF SEVERAL BALLS TO ONE HOLE.

So much of the way we think about golf is dictated by the economics of the game. Rounds are sold to us in eighteen-hole or nine-hole increments—what if we only want to play five holes? The same happens in practice. We've already discussed how many players fall into the trap of thinking they have practiced simply because they hit a bucket of balls when in fact all they did was hit a bucket of balls—and paid $15. One of the most amusing ways in which we let the economics of the game dictate our approach to the game can be seen in how we practice putting.

Why do you think most people practice putting by walking onto the practice green, tossing down three balls, and putting them to one hole? Could it be because golf balls are sold to us in sleeves of three? We buy a sleeve before a round, take them out, and mindlessly putt them while we wait to tee off. Ever notice how often you putt one ball and miss low and then another and miss high and then make the third? Ever joke that the game would be easier if we could hit every shot three times? It would be easier, but that is not the way it is played. Practice your putting the way the game is played.

There are a couple of ways you can do this. The first way is to take one ball and putt it to one hole and then putt at a different hole, working your way around the green. This will make you consider each putt. It will make you think about what you are doing. As part of this process you should also hit a forty-foot lag putt, mark the ball, and then make the putt you have left. Another variation on this method—one used by Phil Mickelson—is to take six or eight balls and make a circle around a hole about eight feet out. Then work your way around the circle. Each putt will be slightly different than the one before. You can add to the pressure of the situation—and thus more closely simulate real golf—by saying that you will continue the drill over and over until you make all eight in a row. Putting the same putt over and over actually hurts your putting by allowing your brain to get lazy. Study each putt anew.

CHIP AND THEN PUTT.

This is the most realistic way to practice your short game. Chip to a hole and then make the putt. Add more pressure to the drill by setting a specific goal for yourself. We can't tell you what that goal should be. It should be whatever is challenging for you. Most players practice chipping—hitting the same chip three times at the same hole—and then practice putting, stroking three putts at the same hole. Instead, practice your up-and-downs. This is the way it will happen on the golf course. Get good at something that matters. This exercise not only disciplines the mind, but it will condition the body to react to the feel of different clubs in your hand. By changing clubs before putting—going from a wedge to the putter—you have simulated what happens in real golf. You will be teaching yourself not just the shots involved, but also to make the transition from one kind of shot—a chip—to another kind of shot—a putt.

CREATE A PAR-2 COURSE
AROUND THE PRACTICE GREEN.

Take one ball and play from nine different positions around the practice green. Give yourself some challenging up-and-downs—including bunker shots if you can—and concentrate on making up-and-down saves. It is those saves that knock strokes off your scores. At first, you can keep your focus by seeing how you shoot in relation to the par of 18 on the nine-hole course. Later you can focus your practice in the same way you did with your putting: Set as a goal playing nine holes in 18 strokes before you abandon the drill.

Notice how reliably solid professionals are from one hundred yards and in. They have prepared their minds and their games to get up-and-down when they are inside one hundred yards. By creating a par-2 course you will not only learn the shots you need to get up-and-down, but you will also develop the belief in yourself needed to get up-and-down.

The one thing we want to emphasize is that INTENTION

must equal ATTENTION. You first need to be clear about your intention (purpose) for playing golf. For most of you the intention is to score lower. What does that mean? Simply put, to get the ball in the hole in as few strokes as possible. Therefore, enough practice time is needed to focus ATTENTION on that INTENTION. That means to SIMULATE GOLF. As we said above, this is done by focusing on a target, using different clubs, using different lies, following your routine, trying different shots, and adding some pressure. ATTENTION is about where you put your focus, where you direct your energy.

We usually say to make sure to simulate golf at least 50 percent of your practice time. If you don't have any smaller intentions to work on, you can do it 100 percent. Smaller IN-TENTIONS can be to improve distance response in putting or your technique in pitching, or to work on your aiming or post-shot routine.

While the overall goal of practice should be to simulate real golf as closely as possible, there are, within practice, three different types of practice.

1. **MAINTENANCE PRACTICE**—This focuses on the nuts and bolts of the game. This is where you make certain that you have not gotten sloppy with basics such as ball position, tempo, aiming, and alignment.

2. **PERFORMANCE PRACTICE**—It can be preparing for a tournament when you might be extra nervous, or playing with a partner who is extra talkative. How can you prepare for it? It can also be preparing for unusual circumstances. Perhaps you are going to Scotland and need to get ready for a

links course or are going to Florida and will be playing on Bermuda grass. Maybe you are going to play on an unusually tight course and need to work on hitting fairways with a 3-wood off the tee.

3. **FUTURE PRACTICE**—This involves building all those skills that will help grow your game. Maybe it's learning a new shot, or maybe it is working on managing your emotions.

These are all different and valid forms of practice. But within these forms of practice a purpose must always be present. Don't let your mind wander. Don't do it by rote or just walk through the motions. Make yourself be there, make yourself be in the now. **Great play begins with thoughtful practice.**

There is also a difference between warm-up and practice. The INTENTION for warm-up for most players would be to warm up and get in a state of confidence with body, swing, and mind. How do you best accomplish that? How can you do it in five minutes or in forty-five minutes? Many players set themselves up for failure even before the round. If you, for example, need to hit the ball perfectly in warm-up to have a good round, you are setting yourself up for trouble.

We frequently play games with our students to get them to think more about how they practice. We tell them that they can practice anything they want, but that every shot they hit on the range must have a purpose. Almost always what we hear back is that they have never hit so few balls on the range and been so exhausted. Once, working with the University of

New Mexico team, Lynn talked about practice quality. The team decided that for a month they could play—but they could not go to the range and scrape-and-hit. The result? The next match they played, they had their lowest team total. And then what did they do? They all ran to the practice range. Some habits are hard to break.

PRACTICE PLAN THINKING

What do you want to have accomplished after the practice session?

How much time do you have?

What practice resources are available?

How and for how long will you simulate golf during this session?

How can you keep the best possible attention on your intentions for the practice session?

EXAMPLE:

Two-hour maintenance practice

Main intentions: swing and distance response in putting and pitching

Warm up body and swing—fifteen minutes

Check swing change in mirror—fifteen minutes

Two different putting distance exercises—about thirty minutes

Swing tempo exercise—fifteen minutes

Distance pitching—thirty minutes

Simulate golf on the range—fifteen minutes

We hear many people say that they do not have the time required for the amount of practice it takes to get good at golf. We say that if you practice with a purpose it won't take nearly as much time as you think. You can gain a lot more from thirty minutes of simulating real golf on the range than you can from two hours of mindlessly hitting balls. If the purpose of practice is to perform better on the golf course, then doesn't it make sense to make practice look and feel like real golf? Otherwise all you are doing is making yourself into one of those people who, midway through a round, will lament: "I've been hitting it so well on the range." Exactly. Too bad that's not real golf.

CHAPTER XI

Play with a Purpose:
Don't Try a Shot You Can't Handle

"Don't try shots beyond [your] ability, and don't get upset on the course."

—JOYCE WETHERED, FIVE-TIME ENGLISH
WOMEN'S AMATEUR CHAMPION

SWING KEY: Good shots are a combination of commitment, trust, and honesty.

We have talked a lot about imagining the impossible and then figuring out how to make it happen. The belief that everything is possible will make us better in all that we do in life. But it is also important to remember that perfection is not an accident, but rather the result of hard work. Annika Sorenstam did not shoot a 59 merely because she had the vision to imagine that it was possible, and Tiger Woods did not win four consecutive major championships on imagination alone. What both Annika and Tiger have developed—along with their games—is an astute sense of assessing risk/reward situations on the golf course.

When Tiger first came onto the pro tour, his greatest strength was also his greatest weakness: He believed in his heart of hearts that he could do anything. While that belief led him to work magic at times, at other times it also led him to double and triple bogeys. It took him a while to develop the discipline NOT to try the hero shot all the time. Tiger emerged as the player who dominated from 1999 through 2002 when he learned something that Jack Nicklaus knew very well. In competitive golf, you don't always NEED to shoot a 65. In other words, don't try the hero shot unless you have to be a hero. Those players who have been the most successful in major championships—Woods, Nicklaus, Sorenstam, Faldo, Hogan, Jones—all developed a plan to minimize their own mistakes while waiting for their opponents to make mistakes.

The key to more thoughtful golf is to expand your choices. The more options you have available to you, the more likely you are to find the right choice for the situation at hand. **One of the miracles of merging the mental and the physical in the game of golf is that you will find that, by playing within your ability, you can exceed your expectations.** One of the most common mistakes of average golfers is that they make decisions based on their best shots rather than on their usual shots. Notice that most misses to greens are short and right. Maybe you should play a round in which one of your goals—your PLAYING FOCUS—is that you are going to get every approach shot past the pin. **Remember, achieving the impossible is merely stringing together a series of the possible.** It's crucial to discipline your mind to evaluate the situation and determine the best possible shot to hit. Sometimes bogey is a good score.

How can you learn to expand your choices on the golf course? We have several drills you can take out onto your home course that will put you in better touch with your creative side. Play nine holes on your home course with the intention of being extra aggressive. Take out the driver on every hole, go for every pin. What does that feel like? Now play the same nine holes and be more strategic. Tee off with a 7-wood or a 5-iron and play for the middle of the greens. What did you learn from this drill? From your competence level, how would you play the holes with the shots you are best at?

On another occasion, play nine holes on your course with the purpose being to go for the front of the greens, then play nine holes going for the back edge of the greens. What did you learn from that? Play nine holes hitting fades and draws off the tees and into the greens. What seems to work best? Remember, golf is about getting the ball in the hole in the fewest number of strokes. What works best for you and the courses you are playing? The more choices you have, the greater your chances for success. Like the person mindlessly banging balls on the practice range, many players get stuck doing the same thing over and over again, either being overly aggressive or overly conservative. The more you expand your repertoire the sweeter your performance will be.

One of the most disciplined bits of thinking under pressure

came from Nick Faldo on the last hole of his singles match against Curtis Strange in the 1995 Ryder Cup. The point at stake in their match was crucial, and they were all square when they drove off the eighteenth tee. Faldo hit into the gnarly rough. Knowing he needed to make par, Faldo did not panic. He took out a wedge and played a shot to the fairway ninety-three yards short of the green. He then pitched from ninety-three yards to four feet and made the putt. Strange, meanwhile, hit his second shot into the rough on the hill short of the green—exactly the spot Faldo was avoiding. His difficult chip from the high grass ran fifteen feet past the hole and he missed the par putt. Faldo won the hole and the match and Europe won the Ryder Cup. It was not only a brilliant piece of thinking under pressure by Faldo, but it also displayed the confidence he had in his ability to pull off the up-and-down once he laid up to ninety-three yards. It was the mind and body working perfectly together. Faldo was honest with himself about what shot he was capable of hitting from the rough, and he trusted himself to hit the follow-up shot and make the putt. Most importantly, he expanded his choices so that he had a variety of options open to him.

Now think of how the recreational golfer—or even some professionals—would react in that situation. Hitting the ball perfectly and putting it on the green might be possible, but how likely is it? If you can *sometimes* hit the ball 200 yards on the fly and that's how far it is to carry a water hazard, why try it? More often than not you will end up wet. Learn to recognize that a 5-iron off a downhill, sidehill lie is a difficult shot and that maybe the best way for you to make par on the hole is to hit a 7-iron up near the green and then chip up and one putt. Again, so much of this is learning to pay attention to yourself. By understanding your tendencies you can learn to avoid the bad ones and exploit the good ones. Good decision making can keep par alive and push double bogey out of the picture. That's what Faldo did on that eighteenth hole at the Ryder Cup.

The only time you need to try to make magic happen is when magic is the ONLY solution to the problem. Phil Mickelson was 0 for 40 in major professional championships employing an attacking style that featured an infatuation with distance (he loved hitting the 320-yard tee ball) and a similar infatuation with some shots he could hit better than anyone else (his flop shot comes to mind). It is certainly not a coincidence that when Mickelson finally won his first major—the 2004 Masters—it came when he employed a strategy in which he abandoned the hard hook with the driver for the controlled fade with a 3-wood off the tee. He left the sixty-degree wedge in the bag and played bump-and-run shots and even some putts from the tight lies of the chipping swales that surround the Augusta National greens. In short, Mickelson won when he put his ego aside and developed a more realistic assessment of all the shots he had available to him that he could use to win that tournament on that golf course.

Most of you reading this are not playing in major professional championships and you may not be playing Augusta National Golf Club, but you can bring the same approach that Mickelson used to win the Masters to the courses you play. Say that on the third hole you have driven the ball into the right trees and you have 170 yards left to the green. The trees block a straight path to the green, and the only way you can get the ball on the putting surface is by striking the ball perfectly off a less-than-perfect lie and then fading it a good ten yards. If you miss you will be, at best, in a bunker and, at worst, in the rough having to chip over the bunker to a short-side pin.

Perhaps the highest-percentage way to make par is to advance the ball on the safest aggressive line—perhaps getting it to within forty yards of the green—and then trying to make an up-and-down from there to save par. At the very least, you are likely to have taken double bogey out of the equation. Sure, you are capable of hitting the hero shot out of those trees, but do you need to right now? How many times have you tried to hit a shot like that only to hit a tree and end up making a seven? Then, as you walk to the next tee, instead of thinking of the drive you have to hit, your mind is ruminating on why you didn't just play the safe shot and make a bogey. If it was the last hole and you were 1-down, then the gamble would be worth the risk.

What we are asking you to do here is to challenge yourself with this question: Do I think about how I am going to play a hole and how I am going to play a shot? It is so very simple to fall into the lazy habit of sticking the tee in the ground, placing the ball on it, and whaling away. This goes back to the basics of our approach. Plan the shot. Commit to the plan. Hit the shot. **Good shots are a combination of commitment, trust, and honesty.**

Part of the decision making that occurs in the THINK BOX involves an honest evaluation of the risk/reward situation inherent in the shot you are about to play. When a player is criticized for not performing well under pressure, attention is usually focused on the player's physical performance. Did they make a good swing? Television cameras will show us replays of the angle of descent into the ball or capture how the hips may be bailing out at impact. Too often overlooked is the mental mistake that may have contributed to the poor shot. Certainly, making the proper decisions on the golf course is at least as important as executing the proper swing.

One of the overlooked aspects of what we cruelly call "choking"—and all of us who have played the game have choked on a shot at one time or another—is poor decision making. When the mind is swept away by a body flooded with adrenaline in a pressure situation, bad decisions are made. One of the reasons it is important to evaluate your play after a round of golf is because not all of our bad decisions are made at crucial times in a round. Strokes can be thrown away on the third hole when you tried a low-percentage shot.

Good decision making on the golf course—like a good swing—is a learned behavior. It doesn't simply happen but needs to be worked on. Go over a round after you have played and distinguish between strokes you frittered away because of poor shotmaking and strokes you frittered away because of poor decision making. When you learn to recognize poor decisions after the fact, you will have taken an important step toward avoiding those poor decisions in the heat of competition. Learn more shots so you have more decisions available to you.

Again, one of the things that traditional golf instruction

does not teach us is how to develop our mental approach to the game. When we step into the THINK BOX, we need to make a shot selection that is based not only on the physical challenge facing us but also on the emotional challenge. Remember, for success to occur in the PLAY BOX, we must cross the DECISION LINE with full confidence that we can pull off the shot we are about to try. When you leave the THINK BOX, leave doubt behind. **If trust is the key to performance, then honesty is the doorway to trust.**

You will be your best coach on the golf course when you are the most honest with yourself in your shot selection. It does not work to simply say, "I am going to play smarter golf." Shot selection is something that needs to be worked on and developed, just as good touch around the green is cultivated by focused practice and the experience of play. Make self-evaluation a priority. Make focused thought a goal. This sort of controlled thinking process is exactly what we are talking about when we refer to PLAYING FOCUS. You can make yourself a smarter player, and you can learn to avoid shots you can't handle. It's all found in the THINK BOX.

CHAPTER XII

Send Your Mind on Vacation

"Feel at ease, lack worry, and no guessing as you hit the ball."

—WALTER HAGEN, FIVE-TIME WINNER
OF THE PGA CHAMPIONSHIP

SWING KEY: Get out of your own way and let good golf happen.

Just as many different kinds of swings work on the golf course, so also do many different kinds of personalities function successfully. Just as with the swing, the important part of on-course behavior is to be true to who you are. That is not to say that a temper tantrum can produce good golf. Inappropriate behavior is rarely rewarded with success. But the notion that you must grind in full concentration the entire time you are on the golf course works for only a few people. If that is not your personality, don't try to make it be

your personality. The key is to find the inner calm—your coherence zone—in which your mind and body can most easily
function in harmony.

We have all heard the stories about how Ben Hogan walked
the course in a world of his own, rarely speaking to his playing
partners. One such story tells of a man Hogan was paired with
in the Masters making a hole-in-one on Number 12—the fa-
mously difficult par-3 at Augusta National. The ball went in
the hole and Hogan said nothing. The two men walked to the
green and Hogan said nothing. The man retrieved his ball
from the hole to the ovation of the gallery and still, Hogan
said nothing. After Hogan knocked in a putt for a 2, the two
men walked to the thirteenth tee with still no acknowledg-
ment from The Hawk about the hole-in-one. After they both
drove from the thirteenth tee and started walking down the
fairway, Hogan said, "You know . . ." and the man swelled
with pride, assuming the great Hogan was about to congratu-
late him on the hole-in-one. But then Ben finished his sen-
tence: "That's the first birdie I've ever made on that hole."

While Hogan went about his work with barely a word to
his playing partners, totally lost in self-absorbed concentration, Lee Trevino was a constant stream of chatter. Once, in
an eighteen-hole U.S. Open play-off with Jack Nicklaus,
Trevino was told by Nicklaus on the first tee, "Lee, there will
be no talking today." Without missing a beat, Trevino responded: "Don't worry, Jack. You don't have to talk, just listen." Both men were very capable of being true to their
personalities on the golf course.

Arnold Palmer played off the energy of the gallery and

Tiger Woods responds to great shots with emphatic fist pumps and whoops of joy. Jesper Parnevik escapes the pressure of the moment by doing complicated math problems in his head as he walks along. And Nick Faldo would sing to himself on the course. All were finding what worked best for them.

What happens with a lot of golfers—from seasoned professionals to the most casual recreational player—is that when they are under the pressure of concentration, they try to become someone other than who they really are. The results are almost always disastrous. The perfect melding of the mind and body—like the perfect grip on the club—is not something forced but rather a state that is allowed to happen. If you do not learn this, it will show up on the scorecard as a blow-up hole. And you can learn this. It is all about energy management and composure. This is an achievable state, not an elusive commodity.

The mind, like the body, works best when it is relaxed. If it is not your personality to disappear into the silence of concentration, then it is literally possible that you can think yourself into failure. This kind of constant grinding consumes energy. Believe in the routine you have developed, and be who you are. Get in the THINK BOX, then get in the PLAY BOX. In between, let your mind relax. Talk with your playing partners—or even your opponent—if that is the way you would normally behave. If you start to feel the pressure of the competition growing inside you, one tool many of our students have found useful is to send their mind on vacation between shots. One way to do this is to think about something enjoyable in your life that is coming up.

When Annika shot her 59 in the second round of the Standard Register Ping tournament in 2001, she was barraged with attention from the fans, the media, other players, and tournament and tour officials. By the time she got to the final round, between the demands and the excitement she hadn't slept for two nights and was both exhausted and concerned that she would not be able to hold onto her lead. She very much did not want to devalue the 59 by not winning the tournament. Pia spoke with her the morning before the final round and Annika said that she just did not have the energy to play a five-hour round of competitive golf.

So Pia asked her: "Do you have the energy to play for thirty minutes?" Annika said that would not be a problem. So Pia pointed out to her that her pre-shot routine in the THINK BOX takes about twenty seconds and that she spends about five seconds in the PLAY BOX. If she is going to play seventy shots that day, then she is spending only about a half hour actually playing golf. Pia told her not to think about being on the golf course for five hours but rather to focus on the fact that she will only need about thirty minutes of actual playing time with breaks built in. Pia told her that what she needed was to send her mind on vacation between shots.

Pia asked Annika what she could focus on between shots to make it more of a vacation and to conserve energy. Annika decided to focus on what things she could cook the next week and how to decorate a room in her house. They were both pleasant places for her mind to go between shots. Similarly, in 2003, when Patricia Meunier-Lebouc won the Kraft Nabisco

Championship, she said afterward that between shots she visited her thirtieth birthday party held a few months earlier.

Enjoy being on the golf course. Enjoy the beauty of the game and the surroundings, enjoy the company of those whom you are with. When feeling the tension that comes with competitive pressure, find a fun place for your mind to relax between shots. Do math problems. Sing. Count your steps between shots. Feel the sensation under your feet as you walk. Focus on your breathing. Think about something fun that is coming up in your life. Just think about how lucky you are to be playing golf. One of the things we ask our players that has to do with energy management is whether they have as much or more energy walking off the eighteenth green as they did when teeing off on Number 1. If not, maybe there is something you want to do differently. We have some players keep an energy scorecard on which they evaluate their energy level after each hole.

When you arrive at the ball, it is time to get back into the THINK BOX. When you are over the shot, you are lost in the moment of the PLAY BOX. In between, be yourself. This notion completely contradicts the established idea that the mind must think only about golf while on the golf course. Think back on it and you will probably notice that your best rounds have been on days when you were relaxed and having fun. Perhaps it was playing well that made it an enjoyable experience, but it is just as likely that you played well because you were enjoying yourself. **It is on those days that you get out of your own way and let good golf happen**.

While watching our professional students play, we get to observe their amateur playing partners on pro-am day at tournaments. It is fascinating to see how the amateurs react to the pressure of playing with professionals and the pressure of playing in a competition. Frequently, the early part of the round is marked by nervous chatter. The latter stages often fall into an eerie silence as the pressure builds. Nerves lead to chatter early, and fear leads to apprehensive silence later. The successful amateurs in these situations are the ones who are best able to remain themselves during the entire round, fighting the temptation to ride the emotional swing either too high or too low.

The destructive nature of pressure in all aspects of our lives is that it gets us out of being who we really are and transforms us into someone we barely recognize and, oftentimes after the fact, someone we realize is not a pleasant person. How often does the stress of work or family life make you pop off at someone in a way you would not normally? One of the things you have learned in this book is how to be better at recognizing when stress is entering your body. By learning how to send your mind on vacation when confronted with stress, you can become better at dealing with that tension. What comes to mind is the advice Peter Pan gives to Wendy when teaching her how to fly: "Think lovely thoughts," Peter says. It's only when we allow room for inspiration, imagination, and intelligence that we can fly.

All successful golfers have a stress-release technique they employ, whether they recognize it or not. Arnold Palmer's interaction with the gallery functioned as a vacation spot for his

mind. Fuzzy Zoeller whistles as he plays. Both Annika Sorenstam and Tiger Woods have extremely close relationships with
their caddies. Watch their interaction and notice how, many
times after a big shot on the way to the next shot, the player
and the caddie will exchange a few words and then laugh.
Maintaining a sense of humor can be a very useful release
valve for pressure. Pia was once caddying for a student for
whom English was her second language. In a particularly
stressful situation, the player asked Pia for "the wife club." It
was only after a few seconds of confusion that they realized
that she wanted the 5-iron but had lost the English words for
it because of the pressure. The fact that both of them could
immediately laugh about the incident turned a potential negative into a positive.

The THINK BOX is an intense time. The mind must be
focused. The PLAY BOX is a lonely time. It is when you totally commit to your belief in the routine you have developed
and the shot you have selected. But if you spend twenty-five
seconds in the THINK BOX and five seconds in the PLAY
BOX and you hit eighty shots a round, that is only forty minutes of actual concentrated play. The other four hours you
spend on the golf course need not be a grind but rather an
enjoyable walk in the park with lovely thoughts in your head.
Golf does not have to be a good walk spoiled. It should be a
good walk—or a good ride. That is a choice we have the
power to make, a PLAYING FOCUS we have the power to
control.

Greatness is not something you force out of yourself, but
rather it is something you allow to emerge from within you

by getting out of the way. Just as genius is often intuitive, so too is inspired golf. Someone performs well on a test or at work because she has prepared well for the task—and she has managed to let that preparation emerge. There are some students who are not good test takers because, when they are confronted with the pressure of the exam, they are unable to let the knowledge come out of them.

You will perform well on the golf course if you have prepared well through your practice, in your preparation for the round—proper rest and nutrition—and in your pre-shot routine. But your hard work will be to no avail if you do not have the tools to let what you know emerge to control what you do. There is nothing you can do between shots except get in your own way. THINK BOX, PLAY BOX—then send your mind on vacation. It will keep you focused by keeping you relaxed.

CHAPTER XIII

See the Putt from Behind The Ball, Then Trust What You See

"The excellence of anyone's game depends on self control."

—ALEX MORRISON, AUTHOR OF THE 1932 BOOK
A NEW WAY TO BETTER GOLF

SWING KEY: Build confidence by speaking kindly to yourself.

Anyone who plays a musical instrument will tell you that it is more difficult to play slowly than it is to rip off notes in rapid succession. When playing quickly it seems as if the mind surrenders more easily to the body because there is not the time to think. The seamless integration of the mental, physical, and emotional is at its glorious best when we are able to stand aside and allow it to happen. It is when playing notes slowly that the musician can get too self-conscious and lose rhythm and feel. It is the truly gifted musician who can play a slow piece with passion and feeling. And it is the truly gifted golfer who gets better as he or she gets closer to the hole.

The full swing, like the fast musical piece, unfolds with a fluid fury that allows little time for the mind to get in the way. Golf gets more difficult the closer to the hole we get because the tension builds in proportion to expectation. Sometimes it seems as if the hardest putt to make is the one you are expected to make. Proper execution of these shots requires intense concentration. As powerful as Jack Nicklaus was, most observers would agree that what truly separated him from his competition was that he was the best putter of makeable putts in the history of the game. It seemed like he always made those eight-footers. Jack was able to make the expectation of success a command, not a burden. It became his road map and he followed it.

The game unquestionably gets more challenging the closer to the hole you get. It is the half shots, the pitch shots, the putts that require the greatest discipline to keep the THINK BOX and the PLAY BOX separate. There is no area of the game in which players are more likely to lose commitment to the decisions made in the THINK BOX than in putting. How many times do you stand behind a putt, make a decision on the line and speed, and then, when you get over the ball, decide that you are seeing the putt differently and change the line? There is a very simple reason for this.

When you stand behind a putt, you are looking at it straight on, with shoulders square to the hole. Your head is level and you are sensing the break as it actually is. Compare this body posture to the way you are when you get over the ball to putt it. You are hunched over, standing sideways to the hole and, to look at the target, you have to turn your head and squint cockeyed at it. Do you honestly think that you are sensing the break of the putt accurately from a position such as this? Why would you ever trust what you are seeing from this position over what you see when you are standing behind the ball with your eyes and body—and mind!—square to the hole?

Among the reasons the long putter has gained such popularity is the fact that the player, by standing more erect, is sensing the break more accurately than from a hunched-over position and is less likely to make a last-minute move to abandon the decision made in the THINK BOX. Putting must be approached like every other part of the game. Get in the THINK BOX, sense the break, pick a line, commit to it, make your practice strokes in the THINK BOX, and then cross the DECISION LINE into the PLAY BOX. When you are over the ball, get comfortable, connect to the target, and stroke the ball. What you sensed in the THINK BOX is the accurate line. Never abandon it for the cockeyed view you get in the PLAY BOX. And when the voice of doubt creeps into your head, talk back to it. **Remember, you build confidence by speaking kindly to yourself.**

As important as putting is—there is no club you use more often than the putter—it is also the area of the game in which we can get the sloppiest with our practice routine. Most often we just walk onto the practice green, throw down three balls, and start slapping them around. Often we don't even bother to look at the line, instead getting the read from our missed putts. So goal number one in your approach to practicing putting has to be this: Simulate putting like it is in the game of golf. Within that crucial framework you can work on the smaller intentions, like technique, aiming, distance response, reading greens, and tempo. Perhaps most important is to practice the THINK BOX/PLAY BOX routine. Just as golf requires soft hands, putting requires slow eyes. Take the scene in casually, calmly—feel the rhythm of the stroke—not with darting eyes and a racing mind.

Here's what a putting practice session could look like:

AIMING

This goes back to understanding your tendencies. It may be that you consistently line up a little left of your intended line, for example. What you need to do is announce your target— perhaps mark it with a tee—then get in your play position over the ball on ten different putts and have someone check your alignment, or check it yourself with a triangle device that points to where you are aiming. Poor alignment not only gets the ball started on the wrong path, but it can also contribute to other problems. Very often we compensate by changing the path of the stroke.

DISTANCE RESPONSE

Again, this is a one-ball routine. Pick a target, prepare, and putt—except, just as you stroke the ball, close your eyes. Keep your eyes closed until you think the ball has stopped rolling, then say where you think the ball has ended. For example, "I think it is an inch to the right and a foot past the hole." Do this ten times or for a set time frame, like fifteen minutes. Don't putt the same putt over and over. Vary the distance and the line. Also, you can put your glove in the cup so that if the ball goes in you won't hear it rattle around. This will help with your distance control and with your commitment to the putt.

SHORT PUTTS

This drill is one of the few times when it is OK to putt with more than one ball, because in this drill the purpose is to see where the balls end up in relationship to one another. Putt three three-footers with three balls toward a ball marker or coin. The goal here is to roll each ball over the marker or coin and for the balls to end up at a consistent distance past the hole. One of the keys to being a good short putter is consistency of speed. Most short putts are missed because of a jabbing stroke. This drill will help you develop a consistent sense of feel on those three-footers that set your pulse racing.

SIMULATING GOLF

One of the most common problems for shaky putters is not getting the ball to the hole. Often, this player is already thinking about the putt he or she might have next, and is subconsciously just trying to get the ball close rather than actually trying to make it. Here's what you do. Putt nine holes with one ball. Make the putts makeable but not gimmes—maybe in the twenty-foot range. If you make the putt, give yourself three points. If you two-putt, give yourself one point—and putt them all out! No giving yourself any putts! If your first putt is past the hole, but no more than a club length past the hole, you get another point. Arnold Palmer said it: "Never up, never in." This drill will help you become a more aggressive putter.

ROUTINE

As we said, the THINK BOX/PLAY BOX separation is just as important in putting as it is in any other part of the game and, in fact, is even more important because it is so easy to blur the line when putting. There are two components to putting: the line and the speed. Again, as we said, all decisions about the line must be made behind the ball, in the THINK BOX, and while standing fully erect at address. When you get over the ball, connect to the target and focus on the speed of the putt. To make this a routine you follow on the golf course, you must practice it. That is the only way you'll make it a habit.

READING PUTTS/SENSING THE BREAK

Remember, seeing the line is not just a left-brain activity. It requires full integration of the complete self. Be more aware as you are walking to the green of how it is "leaning." When you get to the green, imagine pouring a bucket of water and thinking which way the water would run. One of the most common mistakes we see in players of all skill levels is that they have a good round going and then, all of a sudden, want to break from their routine and start reading the putts for ten seconds longer instead of trusting their sense of the break. This leads to paralysis by analysis. Just because the putt is more important, it doesn't mean you have to take longer to read it. In fact, it is in exactly those situations that you need to trust your routine the most. Stick with what got you there.

Slow play is a curse that can affect not only the future of the game but also the quality of your play. Golf is a game of rhythm, and that rhythm is most easily achieved by eliminating all the distractions that interfere with the integration of the complete person into the game. So many people make practice swings without knowing why. It's almost like they think it is part of the Rules of Golf. If you take a practice stroke in putting or a practice swing on any shot, be clear what your intention is. If it doesn't have a purpose, get it out of your game. The more time- and energy-efficient you can be, the easier it will be to play well over time.

Some people have a clear purpose: They want to rehearse a swing move or get the feel of how hard they want to hit the putt. On a cold day, or if you have been waiting an unusually long time for the group in front of you, you may want an extra swing to help warm up. But be aware of when you are adding practice strokes or practice swings merely to delay hitting the shot. This is a recipe for failure. Too many players confuse playing more deliberately with playing more carefully. In fact, slowing down your play because the shot is more important will not only annoy the group behind you, but will also likely lead to sloppier swings and more missed putts.

We also get concerned for those players who feel that they have to make a perfect practice swing before they hit the shot. That is an extremely difficult burden to play with. What if it doesn't feel right? You are just setting yourself up for a lot of unnecessary doubt and confusion. What is absolutely of major importance in the THINK BOX? Be clear on what you want to do and do it with 100 percent commitment. Take out the rest! Looking at the putt twice as long because it is twice as important doubles the chances for failure.

Watch Annika when she putts. She makes all her decisions in the THINK BOX, takes her practice strokes in the THINK BOX, then gets over the ball, looks at the target, and hits the putt. Golf is not a reaction sport, but we should play it more like it is. Don't play with a sense of urgency, but play with a pace that allows you to feel the game. Play as if the ball will disappear five seconds after you enter the PLAY BOX. Nowhere is that more important than in your putting. See the line, feel the speed, and stroke the ball. It's as simple as that.

CHAPTER XIV

Golf Is About Getting the Ball in the Hole

"Remember, the game is simple. The ball doesn't move. It simply sits and waits."

—BAGGER VANCE, FICTIONALIZED CADDIE

SWING KEY: Keep your ATTENTION on your INTENTION.

The obvious is sometimes, well, so obvious that we miss it. Clichés on this revelation are everywhere. Not seeing the forest for the trees comes to mind. Think about that golf cliché "Drive for show and putt for dough." On the surface, that maxim means that while you impress people with booming three-hundred-yard tee shots, it is often the five-foot putt that wins the match. While that is true, the cliché is even more basic than that. One thing we tend to lose sight of is that the purpose of golf is to get the ball in the hole. Golf is not a game about distance; it is a game about precision. And precision is accomplished by focusing your thoughts.

There are a lot of players who are impressive in every aspect of their game, except when it comes to winning. They drive the ball a long way or are extremely accurate off the tee. They play precise iron shots, have a variety of shots around the green, and putt with astonishing touch. But talent does not always translate into success. It is not so much the ability you have as it is your capability to call on that talent when it is most needed that creates greatness. Phil Mickelson and Greg Norman are men of enormous talent who had trouble winning major championships. Nick Faldo prepared himself so that his talent was at its best when it meant the most. He knew how to get the ball in the hole.

In every sport there are athletes who are referred to as "winners." This sometimes sounds like a backhanded compliment but it is really the highest praise that can be given to an athlete. What is usually meant by calling someone a winner is that they do not necessarily look the best in going about their task, and they may not overwhelm you with their skill level or the polish of their technique, but the bottom line is that they are successful at what they do. In the case of golf, these athletes have achieved a measure of success because they know that the purpose of the game is to get the ball in the hole. It's not about who hits the ball the farthest or who has the prettiest swing. **Winners keep their ATTENTION on their INTENTION.** And the intention in golf is to make the ball disappear into the cup in the fewest strokes possible.

One of the most remarkable tournaments ever played was

the 1986 Masters, when a forty-six-year-old Jack Nicklaus shot a 30 on the back nine on Sunday to win his eighteenth major championship and his final PGA Tour event. It was a day of incredible emotion, and Nicklaus was brilliant at drawing on the positive energy and blocking out the negative distractions. After Nicklaus drove onto the fairway on the final hole and as he walked toward his ball, the incredible outpouring of affection from the fans caused his eyes to start to tear up. Jack caught himself. "I said to myself, 'We still have some golf to play,'" he recounted later. He did not let the moment wash away his focus. He was able to ask himself the essential question: "Am I here right now?" When he realized that he was losing that attention to his intention, he was able to reclaim it. That's what champions do. In short, the genius of Nicklaus was his ability to get the ball in the hole before everyone else. That is what the game is all about.

Faldo once asked Ben Hogan—a four-time winner of the U.S. Open who, from 1940 through 1960, never finished out of the top ten in the national championship tournament—what he needed to do in order to win the Open. Hogan, in what was likely a comment meant to be truthful rather than snide, as it sounded, replied: "Shoot a lower score than everyone else." Is the game really any more complicated than that? Is there someone you play with—and we all know someone like this—who doesn't hit the ball far and doesn't knock down the pins with laser-like iron shots but, just when you think you have the hole won, they are knocking in a seven-footer for par? Those players have not tied their emotional satisfaction to impressing people, just to getting the ball in the hole. Similarly, there are players who will tell you how great they hit the ball that day—but who failed to score well. They have lost sight of the purpose of the game.

One major thing that we want you to learn from this book is to simplify your game by breaking it down into its simplest components. The overriding philosophy—the most CONTROLLABLE GOAL you can have—is to hit every shot with total commitment, to go after it with a complete sense of purpose. We spoke earlier about the point game as a drill to focus your thoughts on the next shot you are about to hit. Here is another drill that will take your mind off the enormity of the challenge—that battle with Old Man Par that Bobby Jones talked about—and focus it on the purpose of the game: getting the ball in the hole.

Like the point game and many of our other drills, this one has the advantage of being a practice technique that can also serve as a game within the game when you are trying to score your best. The more you learn to play these games within the game, the more successful you will be at maintaining concentration. Again, the purpose of this drill is to get your mind in the now and on the task at hand. It will help you build the kind of focus that will enable you to commit fully to your shots and produce more good shots more often—especially when you need them most.

This drill is best done on a course you know well, like your home course or one you play regularly. Sit down with the scorecard and break the layout down into six courses of three holes each. So Numbers 1, 2, and 3 are the first course, Numbers 4, 5, and 6 are the second course, and so on. Decide what

you feel is a fair "par" for yourself on each three-hole segment. Perhaps playing the first three holes one over par is a
good goal for you and shooting two over on the next three
holes is reasonable. With your target scores in hand, set out to
play your "new" course.

When the first three-hole segment is over, just acknowledge to yourself whether you achieved your target score. If
you achieved your target score right on the number, or were
two strokes better than it or one stroke higher, push it out of
your mind and go on to the next three-hole segment. That
first segment is done. It no longer exists. The next three-hole
segment starts with a clean slate. The goal is to see how many
of the six segments you can win. Part of the beauty of this
drill is that it can be tailored specifically to YOU.

Can you see the pattern to our method here? We have
taken an eighteen-hole course and broken it down into six
three-hole courses. We have taken three holes and subdivided
them into single holes on which you can get points for each
shot hit. And we have taken one hole and reduced it—
through the point game and THINK BOX/PLAY BOX—to
one shot: the shot you have to hit right now. Often in life we
are overwhelmed because we focus our attention on the enormity of the task at hand. What we need to do is to reduce the
task to its components, then focus on a specific component as
the most important task at hand.

CHAPTER XV

HEARTGOLF: It All Adds Up to Better Golf

"The heart has its reasons which reason knows nothing of."

—BLAISE PASCAL, SEVENTEENTH-CENTURY WRITER

SWING KEY: Think clearly, and play courageously from your heart.

Have you ever been over a golf shot and your intuition—your heart—was telling you one thing but your intellect—your brain—was singing a different song? Most often what happens in these situations, both in golf and in life, is that the intellect takes control and rules the decision. You make the swing and find out what you already knew: You should have listened to your heart. One of the many ways in which golf mirrors life is the lesson often learned cruelly: that our greatest regrets involve not the decisions we have made that didn't work out, but rather the instincts that we failed to act upon. Acts of true courage, and often pure genius, occur when people follow their hearts.

Pia was coaching a young player who could not make up her mind about entering an upcoming LPGA qualifying tournament. She was not comfortable with how she was hitting the ball and felt that her game was not where she wanted it to be. She made a list of the assets and deficits of her game and was almost convinced that she would not play. At that point Pia suggested that she throw away her list of pros and cons and listen to what her heart was saying. Without a second of hesitation the player exclaimed, "I want to play!" She entered the qualifying tournament and won it, played in her first LPGA event as an amateur, made the cut, and finished in the top 30. The saying may be "mind over matter," but it is the heart that leads you to what really matters.

We believe that for players to reach their full potential they need to learn to listen to both the brain and the heart, and to make decisions based on information from both. We have become "neck ups" when it comes to so many things that we do today. Why do so many players say after they shoot their career low round, "I played out of my mind?" Perhaps the intellect was finally tamed and room was created for the intuitive heart to play the game. This is one of those cases where we are "learning" what we already know. We say it all the time—his heart was in it or she played with all her heart—but we lose sight of that wisdom when it comes time for action. The intellect leads us to what we think is safer ground. That is not where greatness resides.

One of the really compelling things about sports is that they are an immediate window into the essence of a person. In sports, the time frame of normal life is speeded up, and we find out quickly how a person handles pressure and deals with success or failure. We learn a lot about someone in a very short period of time. Perhaps the reason we love to watch a tournament like the Masters is that there is so much heart on the line on the back nine at Augusta National Golf Club on Sunday afternoon. When Jack Nicklaus won in 1986 at the age of forty-six he brushed away tears as he walked to the final green, as did many who watched his remarkable performance. In 1995, Ben Crenshaw pulled off one of the most unlikely Masters victories just days after the death of his lifetime coach and friend, Harvey Penick. Tiger Woods was reduced to tears after his victory in 2005 when he talked about feeling the presence of his ill father with him on the course as he played to his fourth green jacket. These were players whose hearts led them to the higher ground of greatness.

We call this HEARTGOLF®. It's about learning to listen to and follow your heart. The first step along this path for anyone playing the game is to notice what brings you joy as you play and practice. We see this as learning to nurture your intrinsic love for the game separate from score, winning, and outcomes. Sure, we all want to win, but do you still want to get up and practice when things don't go as planned? Tiger Woods said, after his victory at the 2005 Masters, "I don't think you're ever there. You never arrive. If you do, you might as well quit, because you're already there; you can't get any better. I'll never be there." Annika and Tiger share this heartfelt love for developing their excellence and the drive to find the pathway to it.

Here is another example of a guy who figured it out. Lynn was teaching at a golf school and one of the participants came up to her on the last day, gave her a big hug, and said that he had finally figured out how to love the game. Lynn had noticed that this guy loved to hit balls on the driving range, ball after ball—scrape-and-hit, as we call it. He looked like a pig in the mud with his pile of balls surrounding him. Lynn also noticed that when they ventured onto the golf course, he became the incredible shrinking man. He was invisible, not daring to take up any space in the foursome. He didn't come close to playing to his potential. His ball striking was very different from what Lynn had seen on the range. Of course, he had heard that he was supposed to find a purpose to every shot, and he had heard how he was supposed to practice real golf if he wanted to transfer his skills to the course, but he simply could not make the connection.

So what had this guy figured out? He told Lynn, "Well, I'm never going to play golf again!" He had decided that playing golf was not fun for him. What he enjoyed with all his heart was spending the day on the driving range trying to hit the perfect shot. He loved this quest, and playing golf on the course was only a distraction from what was important for him. Yes, this is an extreme example, but the point is this: It is YOUR game, after all. YOU decide what you want to get out of it, and then commit to that decision with all your heart. Certainly, part of what has helped Tiger and Annika separate themselves from their competition is that they have set such lofty goals. That is where their hearts have led them. It is in that pursuit that they find happiness on the golf course. The hard work they put in is not a burden, but a joy.

We want all the players we coach to experience their HEARTGOLF. We see GOLF as an acronym for Game Of Life First, a phrase we first heard from Ken Blanchard, or Greater Optimal Life Focus, which is the name we came up with for it. The purpose is to achieve full coherence in the system, which allows for access to all of our abilities and enables us to achieve our 54. It doesn't mean that you are going to hit every shot perfectly, but it does allow for congruency between the head and the heart, and for clarity and composure to pull off the shot when you most want it. It will help you to think clearly and play courageously from your heart.

In the long run, it's the player who loves the game and all its dimensions who will sustain performance. Research indicates that learning to find and nurture your passion, your purpose for playing, is the intrinsic motivation that sustains you even when the breaks are bad and the scores are high. Find what fun in golf is for you and go for it with all your heart! One technique we coach is called Quick Coherence®. The technique was developed by Doc Childre at the Institute of HeartMath®. It will help you find your heart. Here's how it works:

1. **HEART FOCUS:** Focus your attention on the area of your heart. If this sounds confusing, try this simple exercise. Focus on your right big toe and wiggle it. Now focus on your right elbow. Now, gently focus on the center of your

chest, the area of your heart. If you like, you can put your hand over your heart to help. If your mind wanders (out of habit), just keep shifting your attention back to the area of your heart.

Channeling your attention to your heart may seem like a difficult thing, but that's only because you have never tried it. You've heard the expression, "My heart was in my throat"? Well, now your mind is in your heart.

2. **HEART BREATHING:** As you focus on the area of your heart, pretend that your breath is flowing in and out through that area. This helps your mind and energy to stay focused on the heart area and your respiration and heart rhythms to synchronize. Breathe slowly and gently, in through your heart (to a count of 5 or 6), and slowly and easily out through your heart (to a count of 5 or 6). Do this until your breathing feels smooth and balanced, not forced. It can help to count 1,000; 2,000; and so forth to 5,000 to slow you down and find an easy rhythm. Continue to breathe with ease until you find a natural inner rhythm that feels good to you.

We tell the players whom we coach to do this until it feels completely natural—until you don't have to think about what is going on. Eventually, the rhythm will relax you. You will have to find your own way, but we have found that to exhale twice as long as the inhale helps lower the adrenaline level and seems to help players become coherent more easily.

3. **HEART FEELING:** Continue to breathe through the area of your heart. As you do so, recall a positive feeling, a time when you felt good inside, and try to reexperience it. This could be a feeling of appreciation or care toward a special person or a pet, a place you enjoy, or an activity that was fun. Allow yourself to feel this good feeling of appreciation or care. If you can't feel anything, it's okay; just try to find a sincere attitude of appreciation or care. Once you've found a positive feeling or attitude, you can sustain it by continuing your heart focus, heart breathing, and heart feeling.

Let your mind associate that positive memory with the in-balance way you are feeling right now and make that be a place your body wants to go to.

HeartMath's emotional refocusing technique can get you back on track when you are unraveling on the golf course. It can also help in any area of your life when day-to-day stress threatens to throw you off track. Use this technique before meetings, or while driving, or anytime you want to approach a task with better clarity. For our purposes, you can practice this breathing technique on the way to the golf course or as part of your warm-up routine. It can also be used in your pre-shot routine, your post-shot routine, or while waiting to hit on a hole when there is slow play in front of you and the tension is starting to build. This technique will help you overcome fear and anxiety and anger, and will get you back in sync. Try it!

Another wonderful technological breakthrough achieved

by the folks at HeartMath is the use of the Freeze-Framer®
Interactive Learning System. It's used by everyone from mili-
tary pilots to competitive athletes of all sorts to improve
hand-eye coordination, manage emotions, and improve focus.
Today it is very popular to view your golf swing on video and
see in detail with graphics showing what your swing is actually doing. We agree with the saying that a picture is worth a
thousand words, but can you experience the benefit of a good
golf swing if you are in an emotional state where you can't
perform it? Peak performance requires both a coherent swing
and coherent heart rhythm. We think it's just as important to
see what your emotions are doing. The Freeze-Framer software
allows you to see in real time what your emotional state is.

The Freeze-Framer is a simple, easy-to-use interactive software program that displays your heart rhythms and shows you
how stress may be affecting you. Using the fingertip pulse
sensor that plugs into a port of your computer, you can watch
in real time how thoughts and emotions affect your heart and
autonomic nervous system. You will learn how to intentionally shift to a positive emotional state and will be able to see
the changes in your heart rhythms immediately on your computer screen. These shifts in your heart rhythms create a favor-
able cascade of neural, hormonal, and biochemical events that
benefit the entire body and mind. Blood pressure drops. Stress
hormones plummet. The immune system pumps up. Anti-
aging hormones increase. You gain clarity, calmness, and control. The effects are both immediate and long-lasting.

The Freeze-Framer is an education system that shows a
person's heart rhythm patterns, which in turn allows them to

see and better understand how stress and emotions are affecting their autonomic nervous system dynamics. It does this by measuring the naturally occurring changes in beat-to-beat heart rate, which is called heart rate variability (HRV) analysis, or simply, analysis of the heart rhythm. Research has shown that sustained positive emotions lead to a highly efficient and regenerative functional mode associated with increased coherence in heart rhythm patterns and greater synchronization and harmony among physiological systems.

As people practice coherence-building techniques, they can readily see and experience the changes in their heart rhythm patterns, which generally become more regular, smoother, and more sine wave–like as the individual enters the coherent mode. This process enables individuals to easily develop an association between a shift to a more healthful and beneficial physiological mode and the positive internal feeling experience that induces such a shift. (To order Freeze-Framer, go to *www.golf54.com* and click on PRODUCT54.)

The Freeze-Framer is very different from devices that simply measure heart rate. It measures the subtle beat-to-beat changes in your heart rate and shows you the rhythmic patterns over time. The Freeze-Framer also analyzes your heart rhythm pattern for coherence, which other HRV monitors do not do. In addition to showing your heart rhythm in real time, your coherence or entrainment level is displayed as an accumulated score.

While certain rhythmic breathing exercises can induce coherence, research shows that increased benefits are achieved by actively adding a positive feeling such as appreciation, love, compassion, and so on. Generating a positive emotion makes it easier to sustain coherence for longer periods, even during challenging situations. Sincere feelings of love and appreciation have a much wider range of health and wholeness healing benefits than simply forcing the system into coherence with breathing techniques alone. Learning to send feelings of love and appreciation through your system while breathing through the heart adds a dynamic set of benefits to emotional self-management and performance. Many describe their cumulative subjective experiences as an increased ability to "live more from the heart" in alignment with their core values.

The heart is a primary generator of rhythmic patterns in the human body, and possesses a far more extensive communication system with the brain than do other major organs. In addition, the heart plays a particularly important role in the generation of emotion. With every beat, the heart transmits complex patterns of neurological, hormonal, pressure, and electromagnetic information to the brain and throughout the body. As a critical nodal point in many interacting systems—physiological, cognitive, and emotional—the heart is uniquely positioned as a powerful entry point into the communication network that connects body, mind, emotions, and spirit.

The Institute of HeartMath Research Center conducts clinical studies and research on emotional physiology and heart-brain interactions, as well as research on the physiology of learning and performance. That research has shown that emotions are reflected in our heart rhythm patterns. These patterns are transmitted from the heart to the higher brain centers, and have profound effects on the way the brain processes information. Feelings of frustration and anxiety cause the heart rhythms to become more disordered and irregular, which inhibits the higher brain centers, causing energy drains, insecurities, and glitches in your decision-making functions. Intentionally generated feelings of love and appreciation, on the other hand, progressively increase your ratio of access to clear and effective thinking, problem-solving discernment, and memory recall, and an increase in your visual acuity. This is because emotions of high quality produce more ordered and coherent heart rhythms, which reduce nervous system chaos and facilitate cortical function.

During states of psycho-physiological coherence, our inner systems function with a higher degree of synchronization, efficiency, and harmony that correlates with improved emotional stability, quality of emotional experience, health, and cognitive performance. Institute of HeartMath studies conducted across diverse populations have associated increased psycho-physiological coherence with reduced anxiety and depression, decreased physical symptoms of stress, enhanced immunity, reduced cortisol, and increased DHEA or dehydroepiandrosterone.

The analysis of HRV, or heart rate variability, is recognized as a powerful, noninvasive measure that reflects heart-brain interactions and autonomic nervous system dynamics, which are particularly sensitive to changes in emotional state. Research showing how emotions are reflected in the patterns of our heart rhythms has led to a new model of emotion. This model includes the heart, brain, and nervous and hormonal systems as fundamental components of a dynamic, interactive network that underlies emotional experience. The Institute of

HeartMath has provided scientific evidence that the heart is truly part of the emotional system, which most people have intuitively known all along.

To learn more about HeartMath you can visit their sites at *www.heartmath.com* or *www.heartmath.org.*

Golf is a challenging game. That is part of our fascination with it. There is no other sport that so closely mirrors life. Unlike the reactive sports where you are running and jumping and responding almost entirely on impulse, golf happens at the speed of life. That creates a set of challenges that are different from any other sport, but not so different from our everyday lives. In truth, it is not an overstatement to say that learning to be a better golfer involves learning to be a better person.

Bad shots happen in golf. Bad things happen in life. The key to success in each is in how you react to those disappointments. Despite all your preparation, despite all your practice, and despite all your hard work, you do not have total control over what happens to you. That's just simply the way it is. What you *can* control is how you react to what happens to you. That's the key to not only a successful game of golf, but also to a successful life.

CHAPTER XVI

Make Pressure Your Friend

"You gain strength, courage, and confidence by every experience in which you really stop to look fear in the face. You must do the thing which you think you cannot do."

—ELEANOR ROOSEVELT, FIRST LADY, 1933–45

SWING KEY: Embrace your fears and drown them in kindness.

In comparing notes about the similarities of the pressure of playing competitive golf with other types of performance, we asked a friend who is a concert pianist if he has ever gotten to the point where he no longer gets nervous when he plays in front of people. "I have not gotten to where I no longer get nervous," he said, "but I have gotten to where I know what it feels like to be nervous. Now, instead of reacting fearfully, I react as if the nervous sensation is an old friend coming to visit." This is a crucial insight about performing well under pressure: We don't conquer fear by pretending that it doesn't exist but rather by recognizing it, embracing it, and dealing with it.

We spoke earlier about the 1996 Masters, in which Greg Norman started the final round six strokes ahead of Nick Faldo and finished it five strokes behind him. In interviews conducted nearly a year after that round, Faldo was able to speak freely about his fears that day, acknowledging that he was so nervous that he had to drink water on every hole of the back nine because his mouth was dry from tension. Norman, on the other hand, was never able to acknowledge his emotions. Even twelve months after the fact, Faldo was much better than Norman at admitting the difficulties of the day. Faldo was likely better at dealing with fear because he not only recognized its existence but also accepted it as normal.

While having the courage to admit fear is more difficult than it seems—wouldn't life be easier if we were able to confess to our fears in all social situations?—coping with fear can be easier than we imagine. Let's get back to our music comparison. The nine-year-old daughter of a friend was to have a music recital. About ten students were to play that day and Hannah was seventh in line. When the first child sat down to play, taking out her music, a look of panic spread over Hannah's face. She said to her mother, "I forgot my music." Her mother ran out of the recital, rushed home, got the music, and returned before it was Hannah's turn to play.

When it was finally time for Hannah to perform, she sat down at the piano, opened her music, and flawlessly played three pieces—never once turning a page of the music. The fact was that, through practice, she was completely prepared to play the pieces. But the fact also was that she did not want to deviate from her routine of having the music in front of her. She wanted to step into the PLAY BOX in exactly the manner in which she was used to entering it. Just as importantly, she was recognizing the potential demons around her and taking every precaution to hold them in check. Trust in her routine was how she handled fear.

Acknowledging that fear exists is a positive step. Believing in your preparation to perform is an essential step. As we said earlier, nothing sabotages a swing more than tension, and nothing creates tension more quickly than lack of preparation. The purpose of all of our drills is to develop a routine that focuses your thoughts on the task at hand—the next shot—and relaxes the mind by giving it the belief that you are prepared to perform.

The last day of the 1996 U.S. Women's Open is one of the best examples of putting into practice the tools you are learning in this book. Annika had a three-stroke lead, but a wave of panic came over her right before she was going to tee off. She told Pia that she was so nervous she couldn't sleep and asked, "Can you play for me instead?" Pia tried to ease the tension by joking, "I'll talk to the officials and see if they can change the pairings." But then it became clear that mere humor was not going to be enough. Annika was on a downward spiral. She said that she was afraid she would do the same thing Norman had done in the Masters just months earlier.

Turning serious, Pia said, "I'm glad you are nervous. It

means you care. It would not be normal if you were not nervous. You need the adrenaline from that nervousness to perform today, but maybe it is a little bit too much."

Pia told Annika to travel far away from Pine Needles Golf Club, to go to the moon and look back at Earth. From that perspective, the golf course and the tournament are insignificant dots. "If you shoot 65 or you shoot 85, in one hundred years who will care?" Pia said to Annika. Then, in her first relaxed moment, Annika asked: "Isn't it a little bit important?" Now Pia and Annika were able to settle down and talk.

Pia asked Annika what happens to her mind and body and game when she gets nervous, and Annika responded that her tempo gets quick. So Pia asked what Annika could do to control that situation. Annika said, "I can walk slower, I can talk calmer, and I can take deep belly breaths between shots." Annika also said that her other tendency under pressure is to think too much. She decided that anytime her mind started racing out of control with thoughts, she would chant to herself, "Fairways and greens, fairways and greens."

Annika shot a 66 in that final round and won the U.S. Women's Open by six strokes. Pia walked with the gallery and was in tears as she watched the heart and courage Annika displayed in trusting her tools and using them. After the victory, many people described Annika's play—she hit fifty-one of fifty-six fairways that week in a near-flawless performance—as robotlike and marveled at how nothing affects her. Little did they know how many tools she pulled out of her bag in the final round to insure the victory.

Annika's performance that day was a perfect example of

how combating fear is more than merely an emotional task. Remember, the mind and the body function as one, and when our minds are under stress our bodies react accordingly. While the brain receives the bulk of the credit—and blame—for how we react to situations, the HeartMath research teaches us that to access our greatest potential we need to cultivate more of the heart's intelligence. The more we learn to listen to and follow our heart intelligence, the more our ability to think, focus, learn, and perform increases. The sincere heart passion that Annika showed at Colonial when she played against the men, and at The Solheim Cup in 2003 when she led Europe to victory, was a peek at peak performances that lay ahead.

In this book you are learning the tools that can make you a better golfer. But crucial to the **success** you will have with our approach is the degree to which you **believe** in our approach. The more experience we have with coaching, the more we realize the enormous importance of belief. A belief is simply an interpretation that you hold to be true. Our brains are wired for beliefs and intentions. When activated, the body responds as if the belief was a reality, producing bogeys or birdies, health or illness. Our brains cannot distinguish external from internal "reality." If it is our belief that it is scary to fly in an airplane, then we will be scared every time we fly in an airplane. The only way we can change that fear is to alter the belief.

One thing Pia, Sophie Gustafson, and Annika Sorenstam all had in common as young players in Sweden was their very clear intentions of wanting to be great golfers. All three also had a very strong belief that they couldn't give a victory speech! What did they do? Of course—they made sure they didn't win! It came in the form of missed putts and funky swings and bogeys on the finishing holes. If you didn't know better, you might think their swings didn't hold up under pressure. Now ask yourself: Was it the swing or was it the deep-rooted belief about public speaking? The good news is that each one of these players faced the belief, became aware of how it was limiting their vision, and rewired their brains to give themselves permission to be winners.

When you believe that it is scary to give a victory speech or win a tournament, your heart rate increases just as it would if you were being chased or robbed. For your brain, and thus your heart, this IS reality. In short, our beliefs become our reality. **Change your beliefs and you can change your reality!** Beliefs are a choice. Beliefs give fuel and energy to our intentions. **Embrace your fears and drown them in kindness.** It starts with examining the beliefs we hold true for ourselves as human beings, as golfers, or about the game itself.

When we believe that something is true, our brains command our nervous systems to represent that belief. For all of us, it's high time we become conscious of what we believe in. WHAT ARE YOUR BELIEFS ABOUT YOURSELF, ABOUT OTHERS, ABOUT YOUR SPORT, ABOUT YOUR PROFESSION? What do you want to keep believing in? What beliefs might be good to change? Find beliefs that work for you physically, mentally, and emotionally, and that serve your desires about yourself, your life, and the game. We believe that it's your destiny to believe in something good and something that lasts, but only you know what feels right for you.

When beliefs and intentions are aligned, your greatest potential has room to blossom.

Many different beliefs exist. Check some out for yourself: "Golf is difficult. I'm a great putter. I'll never learn my swing. It's possible to shoot 54. I'm great under pressure. I'm a slow starter. I can't play well without a perfect swing. As soon as I . . ." You have the power to change your world by changing your beliefs.

VISION54 started because of this realization that beliefs limit accomplishment. When Kjell Enhager first suggested it, Pia and her team took it to heart. To believe that we can shoot 54 or lower for eighteen holes was a brilliant shift in worldview, overriding the belief that par is perfection and that every green requires two putts.

In the mid-1990s, Pia and her coaching colleague, Lasse Evertsson, started drawing a tree as a metaphor to explain how all this fits together. Lasse's tree has now been spread thoughout the world! The BELIEFS, values, expectations, culture, and so on are all down in the roots of the tree. As with a real tree, many times it's hard to see the roots or detect them. The trunk of the tree stands for our intentions, and the leaves and branches are our behaviors. The leaves and branches might be things like our fitness, nutrition, body language, swing technique, keeping good stats, inner talk, and the like. This is where traditional coaching is focused. If we focus only on behaviors and neglect our beliefs, the tree cannot grow. Water the root . . . bear the fruit. We believe that the coaches for the future will understand all levels and will give students access to many tools to help them achieve their goals.

As we explore this notion about beliefs, the implications and opportunities are tremendous. Human history is littered with instances when belief was so strong, no challenge to reality was allowed. There was a time when it was thought that the Earth was the center of the solar system, and a time when it was believed that the Earth was flat. More recently, discoveries in quantum mechanics have called into question long-accepted beliefs about Newtonian laws of physics. In all cases, a change in beliefs opened the door to a change in reality. Running a four-minute mile was once thought to be impossible. What we have learned is that the biology of beliefs assures us that the future holds greatness and joy with many one-putts and in which birdies abound! The possibility is there. We just have to believe that it is possible.

It is easier to hang onto our beliefs when everything is going smoothly. In our everyday life, tolerance is tested by adversity. When something bad happens, suppressed prejudices can surface. It is at times like that that we have to be most committed to what we believe.

We all have "off days" and "on days"—those times when we are either out of sync with the world around us or in such a perfect harmony that it feels as if we can achieve anything our hearts desire. What we have to learn to do is to control those off days and cultivate the on days. When you think about it, none of the things we hold dear in life—truth, beauty, love, and knowledge—are places we arrive at, but rather are goals that we move toward. The golf swing is the same way. It is a dynamic, ever-changing process. We pursue its elusive perfection by concentrating on those things we can control: PLAYING

FOCUS, tempo, aiming, confidence, self-talk, and so on. How can you be the best you can be every time you tee it up? By going to your TOOL BOX to change your state. By being AWARE, learning to MANAGE, and daring to CREATE. You can be frustrated and afraid, or you can be motivated and engaged. It is your choice.

What can you do to change your own state while you are out on the golf course? To do that will require keen awareness on your part. We like to think of the ability to change our states as coming from three resources: physical, mental, and emotional. Here are some tools you can check out and add to your "state-managing tool box."

YOU CAN CHANGE YOUR STATE PHYSICALLY.

What happens if you straighten your body posture?

What happens when you keep your eyes on the horizon and above?

What happens when you take deeper breaths from the abdomen?

What happens when you do a few jumping jacks?

What happens when you keep your hands in your pockets?

What happens if you move your eyes more slowly?

What happens if you walk more quickly or more slowly?

YOU CAN CHANGE YOUR STATE MENTALLY.

What happens when you start humming your favorite song?

What happens if you speak in a happy voice to yourself?

What happens when you ask yourself a question like, "What do I appreciate about this round?"

What happens when you focus on something that is under your control?

What happens when you visualize a great shot?

YOU CAN CHANGE YOUR STATE EMOTIONALLY.

What happens when you experience the feeling you had last time you hit a good 5-iron?

What happens when you remember getting a big, warm hug from a favorite family member?

Develop a journal of winning strategies, and keep a record of what goes on when things go badly.

WHAT I DO WHEN THINGS GO WELL:

- My legs feel light.
- I smile and laugh a lot.
- I make clear decisions before hitting.
- I start my warm-up by putting.

WHAT I DO WHEN THINGS DON'T GO WELL:

- I walk and look down between shots.
- I analyze a lot in my head.
- I start thinking about my score while playing.

Now, make your own list!

Keep a notebook in your bag and keep track of it for the next month. What patterns do you see? How can you make sure to use your winning strategies more often? How can you shift things under the negative column to the positive column by using the same state-changing tools?

Learn to make pressure your friend by developing a routine that you believe in and an approach to the game that you trust. Ben Hogan's swing always got better under pressure because he believed in his routine. He trusted it.

CHAPTER XVII

It's All About the Person First

"I have learned, that if one advances confidently in the direction of his dreams, and endeavors to live the life he has imagined, he will meet with a success unexpected in common hours."

—HENRY DAVID THOREAU, NINETEENTH-CENTURY AMERICAN ESSAYIST

SWING KEY: The best golfer you can be is yourself.

Toward the end of Phil Mickelson's 0-for-40 streak in major championships, he was playing in the Bay Hill Invitational shortly before the 2002 Masters. On the sixteenth hole on the final day, Mickelson, trailing by a stroke, drove into some trees on the par-5 hole, whose green is guarded by water. Instead of laying up safely in front of the water and taking his chances of making a birdie from there,

Mickelson hit the high-risk shot and went for the green. What resulted was a ball in the water and the end of his chances to win the tournament.

Mickelson was universally criticized by golf writers, who said the unwise shot that ended up wet was an example of the kind of gambling play Mickelson favored, which would never win a major championship. While it is important to know when to be aggressive, and while it is essential to take advantage of those times when your game is clicking on all cylinders with aggressive play, the truth of the matter is that one of the keys to competing successfully is knowing when to downshift and rein in your game. More tournaments are lost than won, and a car is always under better control in second gear than in fourth. Your career-best score will be the result of a well-managed round as much as the result of a well-played round.

Mickelson responded to the criticism with an interview before the 2002 Players Championship that writers referred to as his "I got to be me" news conference. He said he was only happy when he played gambling golf and that he could play his best only when he was happy. There was a lot of truth to what Mickelson said. Arnold Palmer might have won more than seven major championships if he had played a more conservative Nicklaus-style game, but chances are that the Nicklaus approach would not have worked for Palmer. That wasn't his personality.

It is absolutely essential that you don't separate your golfing self from your actual self. They are the same person, and unless they are totally integrated you cannot play your best golf. Tom Lehman said that Seve Ballesteros played with a body language that said: "No matter where this shot went, the next shot is going to be the best you have ever seen." Lehman said that Nick Faldo's body language said: "I am the only person on the golf course." Both players were masters of what Faldo said was the most important space on the golf course— the five inches between the ears.

The mistake that Mickelson made during all those years of not winning major championships was in not separating the physical approach that was best suited for his personality from the mental approach that would function best under pressure. Hogan played with a style that reflected the grays and whites he wore on the golf course. Palmer, who piloted his own plane and loved to share a laugh and a drink with friends after a round, went at the course in a more carefree manner. But both were able to make wise decisions under pressure and had an ability to understand when to go for a pin and when to lay up because they played within themselves.

Too often, players go out onto the course and try to be someone other than who they are. A normally talkative person becomes quiet and withdrawn because he thinks that is what concentration is. Or a reserved individual tries to spice up her round with Tiger-like fist pumps because she thinks that will release her inner Tiger. The mistake both are making is that they are not being themselves. What we encourage you to do is to find YOUR SWING and YOUR PERSONALITY, then follow OUR APPROACH. The magic of our approach is that we release the athlete inside you who is capable of being a more consistent, higher-performing physical self.

The THINK BOX and the PLAY BOX are the essential duality of the golf course. The key to a successful golf shot is total commitment to the task at hand. Make your decision, believe in your decision, trust your decision—and then act on your decision. But trust must also be built before you get to the golf course. PREPARATION for a round begins with your practice routine and it begins with the manner in which you physically approach competition. Did you get enough sleep? Did you have a proper meal at an appropriate time—for you—before the round? Did you warm up sufficiently?

In our experience of coaching all levels of golfers, building self-esteem and self-worth *separate from performance* is of major importance. In the game of golf, players will always have ups and downs when it comes to performance. It is a natural cycle. The players who cannot keep their self-esteem at a base level during the "down" times have a difficult time sustaining motivation and energy. The pure enjoyment of playing the game, with all of its inherent challenges, wanes. The same goes for our superstars on tour. They also need to be seen for who they ARE, not always for what they DO.

Toward that end, instead of always asking, "Whadya shoot?" try starting your post-round conversation with some of the following questions:

- What did you learn today?
- How was it for you today?
- What experience do you want to remember from today's round?

- Was there any time you became absorbed in the process instead of concerning yourself with your score?
- How was that different for you?
- Tell me about your best experience on the course today.
- What was one of the critical decisions you made today?
- Where and on what did you focus when you were on the course today?
- If you could have done one thing differently in your round today, what would that be?
- How would you like to prepare for your next tournament or round based on what you learned?

The score will always be there on the card, but by shifting your evaluation of the experience from a quantitative outcome to more of a reflection about the process, the opportunity for learning and insight is greatly increased. The answers for the future of your game might reveal themselves as you look more deeply and widely than just at the number you posted. At the very least, it's a more interesting conversation that will produce a healthier perspective about you and your experience in golf. Remember that you are a human being who plays golf, not a golfer who happens to be a human being. **The best golfer you can be is yourself.**

As with everything, self-understanding is greatly enhanced with the proper tools. A tool we have found very useful is the **DISC** personality profile for players. This simple questionnaire will give you an idea who you are on the golf course. Basically, it defines players in four different personality types.

D: These players tend to be left-brained and short-term oriented. Laura Davies is the classic "go for broke" **D** style of play. We have seen Laura "give up" on the last couple of holes if she believes that she is not in contention to WIN. **D** players see the flag and go for it. They have a blind spot for the "sucker pin." They stay engaged with practice only if it's a competition—something they can win or beat someone in. Otherwise it can be boring and they lose intention and attention. Laura sometimes has not known where the driving range was located at a tournament. Once, at a tournament where it was raining, we saw Laura stand under her umbrella watching others warm up, then walk to the tee and shoot 67 without ever hitting one shot or putting one putt. Dottie Pepper's **D** interpretation of the game is reminiscent of General George Patton. She played the Solheim Cup matches with the tenacity of a great warrior in battle. For her, winning is everything! **D**s don't tend to take a lot of lessons. They think they know it all already. They detest slow play. They make their decisions quickly and don't understand what all the fuss is about.

I: These players enjoy the relationships in the game. They seek them out. They organize the breakfast before playing and the party at the nineteenth hole after the round. They would interpret playing alone as boring and not fun. After all, who do you talk to if you play alone? The worst thing for an **I** would be to execute a hole-in-one and not have anyone to celebrate with. In match play, if they get up by a lot of holes, they can feel sorry for their opponent and give away a few holes so the friendship doesn't get lost in the competition. Peter Jacobsen is the quintessential **I**. He loves to play in pro-ams and actually performs better in those conditions. Peter has been known to have the rabbit-ear syndrome and to take a lesson from the guy next to him on the airplane. Jesper Parnenvik is an **I**. He won the Bob Hope and threw a weeklong party for his fortieth birthday for hundreds of his closest friends.

S: These players love the systems and strategies of the game. They seek them out. They want to know the specs on all their clubs or they keep volumes of statistics on their rounds. They like order. You can see it in their golf bag and how they keep everything organized—just in case. They plan and don't like it when the plan gets disrupted—like a flat tire that leaves them late for their tee time and their required warm-up time before a round. They can get stuck in their own system and not nurture the intuitive voice that says it's a 9-iron even though all the data point to an 8-iron. Andy North has won two U.S. Opens and not much else. Par is the system, and par wins U.S. Opens. Par doesn't make the cut at most other PGA Tour events. When Annika was a younger player, Pia wanted her to work on creating different ball flights. Annika turned to Pia and said, "I don't want to do that until I learn to hit it straight from level lies. I'll get to that later." Or, as a young professional, she disliked playing British links-style courses because she couldn't control where the ball ended up. She thought it was unfair. If she hit the ball 152 yards, it was supposed to stay there.

C: The game is complex for these players. They have their own internal evaluation of how it is supposed to be played. They believe that there is a right way to play the game. Embarrassment for a **C** is to make a hole-in-one with a topped shot, or a club that was not what they think is the proper one. They tend to be conservative. They actually think the wood should still be made from wood. They are the "keepers of the game," tending to love the history and lore that surrounds it. They love to play or practice alone because then they can stay internal, which is where they feel most comfortable. They are competent players whose confidence can go up and down. **C**s can leave a day of practice with complete dejection because they didn't accomplish everything perfectly. They need to learn to achieve, then leave. When Fred Couples was the number-one player in the world, he disliked the limelight so much that he once said that when his phone rang at home, he didn't answer it because someone might be on the other end. **C**s want to play the game and go home to their comfort zone. Pia struggled with winning as a junior because she was afraid to speak in front of a group. When **C**s become confident they can appear like **D**s because they have both competence and confidence. Annika is a perfect example of this.

You might have one dominant style or a combination of styles. All of them are great. Nothing is right or wrong. It's all about finding your own tendencies and determining what advantages you can draw from them. As we like to say, anything overused ends up being a weakness. To access more of your potential, your 54, it becomes vital to be honest with yourself, knowing yourself and your tendencies. Realizing VISION54 begins with awareness. **Awareness creates opportunity.** We call it Aware-Manage-Create. To make any change in your swing, attitude, or emotional management, you first need to be aware. After you have become aware of something, you have the option and the opportunity to start managing it and create the future you want.

The beauty of the DISC behavioral model is that it's accurate, it's easy to understand, and the application is immediate. Bobby Foster, former head golf coach and associate athletic director at the University of South Carolina, has created an excellent online mental profile based on DISC, "The Mental Golf Workshop." Go to *www.golf54.com* under PRODUCT54 for the profile.

Understanding exactly who you are will help you develop the routine that works best for you. Ben Hogan would drive to the golf course below the speed limit on the day of a competitive round as a discipline to insure that he would not rush his tempo. In Hogan's mind, a smooth swing began with a smooth ride to the course. We hope that part of what you learn from us is that a method you trust will always be there for you. Sometimes, in match play, a competitor skillful at gamesmanship will try to slow-play a player who plays best when playing quickly, or will try to speed up the pace of play for a player who is deliberate. No matter what is going on around you, you will always have the solitude of the THINK BOX, the certainty of the DECISION LINE, and the physical joy of the PLAY BOX. The more you trust that they will work for you, the more they will work for you.

We were at Colonial Country Club that day in May 2003 when Annika Sorenstam became the first woman in fifty-eight years to play in a PGA Tour event. It could very well be that no one has ever had to hit a single shot with as much pressure on her as Annika did when she struck her first tee ball that Thursday morning with the entire world watching. At risk with that shot was not just what the world would think about Annika Sorenstam, but also what the world would think about women's golf. It was a pressure of which Annika was well aware.

As Annika walked from the practice green to the tee box, Pia approached to give her words of encouragement. Annika was so nervous she could not talk. When she stepped onto the tee and waited for her turn to hit, her caddie, Terry McNamara, said he could see the muscle in her neck pulsing with tension. It was in those last few minutes before Annika hit her first shot in a PGA Tour event that we held our breath, anticipating the ultimate test of everything we had built into our system of preparation.

In their time alone together during the three days of practice at Colonial before the first round, Annika and Terry talked at great length but with great simplicity about that first tee shot. They reduced the approach to this clear thought: Hit the ball and, no matter where it goes, find it and hit it again. Then play the day like any other round of golf. That day, Annika stepped into the THINK BOX with her 4-wood, picked her target, envisioned the ball flight, and then crossed the line into the PLAY BOX. What resulted was a perfectly struck golf shot.

Normally, Annika hits her 4-wood about 220 yards in the air. That day, the ball flew 258 yards. Even with the adrenaline pumping through her, Annika was able to control her emotions by following her plan and by completely trusting that plan. Annika was able to hit that first tee shot at Colonial because she had complete belief in her preparation. She did not try to become anyone other than who she is. Shortly before Colonial, Annika called us and said: "The worst that can happen is that I'll learn something, right?" It was then that we knew she would be all right.

As Annika walked off the tee, she faked a rubber-leg movement that revealed the emotions she was feeling at that time. The magnitude of the moment was greater than any Annika had ever experienced on a golf course, but the key to her success was in knowing that the game plan she had— THINK BOX/PLAY BOX—would work under any conditions. We believe you can learn that belief. When you play with the mind-set that every shot must have a purpose, you will improve. When you accept that it is not about you becoming a golfer but rather about golf becoming a part of who you are, you will play your best.

CHAPTER XVIII

Have a Swing That Suits You

"Use your authentic swing; the one you were born with."

—BAGGER VANCE, FICTIONAL CADDIE

SWING KEY: Trust your swing. It is your signature.

Think of some of the greatest players in the history of the game, players like Ben Hogan, Jack Nicklaus, Arnold Palmer, Nancy Lopez, Lee Trevino, Juli Inkster, and Tiger Woods. What do they have in common—besides success? They each had a unique golf swing that fell short of the textbook way to strike a ball. Hogan's backswing was quicker than normal, prompting Sam Snead to not look when Hogan would swing because he was afraid it would mess up his own tempo. Nicklaus stopped short of parallel, Palmer ducked beneath his follow-through, Lopez had multiple parts to her swing, Trevino had the "caddie cut-swing," Inkster doesn't set her wrist cock until her downswing, and Woods has a hip turn faster than anyone who has ever played the game. The point is, there is more than one right way to swing a golf club. Our main advice about technique is to find what works for you. Your swing is like your signature. It is uniquely yours.

If you can hit the shots you want under pressure, your swing is working. What is important is to make up your mind what swing you believe in, and to have the discipline not to abandon that belief because of a bad round or two. To be in "search-and-scan" mode never works over time. Find your swing, trust it, and stay committed to it. After you decide what you want, it is important to learn to take care of it. We can all fall into bad habits, and there is a certain amount of maintenance practice that we need to do. This involves monitoring things like your grip, aim, posture, tempo, ball position, balance, and so forth. But making a swing change should be done with great care and only after much thought. The reality is that you might get worse before you get better and that it will take time. Even someone as talented as Tiger Woods needed two years of constant work to change his swing. If you are not trained enough in your new swing, the tendency is to go back to your old swing under pressure.

Developing a swing that is mechanically suited to your body type, flexibility, strength, and personality is an important component to achieving your potential. But your body is probably already dictating the kind of swing it needs. We view swing changes as a balance we call "Up-Down." If you are going to get the ball in the hole in as few strokes as possible, you need to plan and consider what you need to develop in yourself, your golf game, and your swing. You need to do the right things in the right way. If you have problems with the driver, good-quality putting practice won't help. When you have decided what needs to be improved, it is important that it really gets done. Many players intellectually understand what they are supposed to change in their swings, but have a hard time actually making the change, and an even harder time making sure it holds up on the golf course in competition.

When Lynn was working with members of the women's golf team at Arizona State University, she helped a player change her swing plane. They practiced all spring and successfully made the change. Then, on the first tee of the NCAA championships, Lynn almost fainted when she saw the old swing show up. When the pressure was on, the player went back to what was comfortable—the old swing. If you decide to get a lesson or some kind of swing coaching a few days before an important tournament, make certain it is just minor maintenance adjustments, like ball positioning, aiming, grip pressure, and other such modifications. Remember, learn your swing and discover how to maintain it. Become aware of your tendencies and check them first when your game goes awry. It's like when an appliance is not working. Check the obvious first. See if it is plugged in.

One problem that we see over and over again is that players of all skill levels are quick to think they need to change their swings just because they have hit a downward cycle in their games. It is extremely important to remember that even in these periods of downward performance, there is learning going on. We are going to have times when we struggle. It is the nature of the game. It happens to everyone, even Jack Nicklaus and Tiger Woods. That does not mean you have to blow up your game and start all over again.

Unfortunately, that is what many players do. They get too impatient when they are struggling and decide that it is time to do a complete overhaul. To them we say: **Trust your swing. It is your signature.**

Making changes during these down periods is usually unnecessary and can be counterproductive. You are likely in a down period because another part of the P+T+M+E+S equation is off. A down period is a time to take inventory of your entire game, not just your swing. Players expect their progress to be a diagonal line moving in a constantly upward direction, but that is not the way learning works. You will have plateaus and dips, and just because you have reached a plateau or are in a dip does not mean you need to start thinking about swing changes.

A couple of things to consider as you venture forward with a swing change:

- Do YOU really want to make the change, or it is something you've read about that sounds good?
- Do you know specifically what it is you want and need to change? There is no room for ambiguity here.
- Do you know HOW you are going to make the change and HOW you will know it is completed?

- What is the specific feedback you are going to use to validate that the change is complete and integrated into your game on the course?

Most players—especially beginners and those recreational players trying to get to the next level—can benefit from pre-swing practice of technique changes. These are things like stance, alignment, and grip. Significant improvement can be made in this area without complete disruption of your game. But in-swing changes—like swing plane—are a much bigger deal and need to be undertaken with a clearly defined purpose.

A friend and colleague, Dr. Bob Christina, is dean and professor emeritus at the University of North Carolina at Greensboro and is also a research consultant for the Pinehurst Company Golf Institute. Bob has this to say about swing changes:

> First of all, pre-swing changes (e.g., widening stance, assuming the correct posture) are usually easier to learn to make than in-swing changes unless the pre-swing changes actually make the swing less fundamentally correct. Before approaching players about learning to make major swing changes coaches/teachers would be wise to answer four questions. First, what is the cause(s) of the swing error(s)? Second, is the player capable (physically, cognitively, and emotionally) of making the swing correction(s)? Third, how long will it take the player to learn to make the swing correction(s)? And fourth, how much will the player's performance be ad-

versely affected while learning the swing correction(s)? One thing that the player needs to understand when learning to make swing changes is that he/she can expect to get worse before he/she gets better.

One technique we use with players of all abilities to gain more awareness of their swing is inspired by Fred Shoemaker. We call it "Tai Chi swings." Have you ever seen that incredibly slow, incredibly graceful hand/body movement that looks like martial arts slowed down to one-thousandth of the speed? That's Tai Chi. A Tai Chi swing is usually performed without a ball at this extremely slow pace—so slow that it should take more than two minutes to complete the entire swing. It takes enormous commitment and concentration to swing a golf club that slowly, but it is well worth the effort.

We have discovered that when players perform their swing this slowly, they come to understand a lot about the overall swing concept and they come to understand just as much about their own physical ability to carry out that concept. It is one thing to intellectually understand what you want to do in your swing and it is quite another thing to be able to do it. Performing it slowly provides superb feedback. If there is a glitch in the swing, it will always show up as a place where the club speeds up involuntarily. As the player becomes more conscious of the tension in different places in the swing, she can then work on these areas. When a player performs the Tai Chi swing with a ball, it's also interesting to observe what is revealed as she starts her forward swing. Her awareness of the "relationship" she has to the ball or to the target is revealed and amplified. Oftentimes, a player who thinks she needs to embark on a swing change will find through the Tai Chi discipline that only minor tinkering is required.

We also feel that players should get involved only in swing changes that they can perform on the golf course. To make a swing change in the smartest way, you need to both simulate golf and focus on the particular part of the swing. We believe it's of no value if a player makes a change on the range but that change does not transfer to the course in competitive conditions. When you do focus on the swing technique detail that you want to change, it needs to be very clear and you must have a specific way to get feedback on whether you are truly enacting the change. The Tai Chi drill might work, or a mirror or video. Be creative in all the ways you can focus on your technique without needing to be on the golf course or the range. Perhaps take an old club, cut it down very short, and put a grip on it. You can use this in your home and have full concentration on the part of your grip, backswing, balance, or swing path that you want to change. When you go to the range, you can spend more time simulating golf.

As we've said, to more efficiently facilitate transfer, it's critical that you simulate golf as you practice. This means that even while you are working on the change in your swing, you will use different clubs, lies, and targets for each swing and shot. You will also commit to your full pre-shot routine with a clear aim to a specific target for each swing. You will also invite the emotion and feeling of pressure as you do this. Simulating the emotional environment you want the swing to hold up under is essential if you want to compete with the new swing. In short, even if you are working on a swing change, it is essential that you practice with a purpose.

As you might suspect, this is a more arduous approach to practice than just making repetitive swings with a 7-iron to the same target without any routine or aim. We can assure you that, if you simulate golf as you practice the swing change, the time it will take for transfer to the golf course will be greatly reduced. We cannot stress enough that we think any form of practice that focuses on just one part of the GOLF54 equation is counterproductive. It goes against all of our knowledge about how people function best.

One more thing we want to mention relative to your process of making a swing change: Please consult with your coach, teacher, or professional and make sure you are physically capable of making the change you seek. An evaluation of your strength and flexibility is paramount. You need to have a swing that your body can make. If you don't like that choice, you need to work with a trainer to get stronger, more flexible, and more in balance. The same is true of your equipment. Many recreational players use equipment ill suited for their body type, strength, or skill level. Check with a professional and make certain you are swinging clubs that work for you. It could very well be that you don't need a swing change as much as you need an equipment change. More likely, what's needed is a belief change. Remember, it is critical to keep attention on the intention. We believe you can play better golf RIGHT NOW without any change to your swing. If you also believe it, then it will be true.

CHAPTER XIX

The 54-Shot Challenge

"You're not obligated to win. You're obligated to keep trying to do the best you can every day."

—Marian Wright Edelman,
American civil rights activist

SWING KEY: It's your world; claim it. It's your game; own it.

Practice will never be the same for you again; at least, we hope that is the case. We hope you have learned that, for practice to be meaningful, it has to be more like real golf. And we hope you have learned that players need to do less tinkering with technique and more tinkering with preparation and attitude. Our exercises are well out of the mainstream, and they work. Not only do they work, but they are also fun, and that should make your practice more productive. If the way you practices ENGAGES you, then you are learning something that will be essential on the golf course: how to stay committed and connected to your next shot.

As we have said before, mindlessly hitting golf balls on the range is not practice, it is merely biding your time. Remember, that poor shot you hit on the seventeenth hole last Saturday to lose a $2 Nassau may have been the result of a bad swing, but what caused the bad swing? Was it poor shot selection? Lack of commitment to the shot? Abandoning your pre-shot routine? All of those? Time spent on the range must be focused not just on how you swing, but also on how you play, how you think. Your mind has to think anew with every shot you hit on the golf course. Why not make it do the same on the practice range?

The 54-shot challenge is likely the most unusual practice drill you have ever come upon. Your first reaction when reading about it will be one of two: You'll either want to run right out and try it, or you'll say it is well beyond your skill level and not for you. While it may seem like the 54-shot challenge is better fitted for the more skilled player, the fact is that everyone can learn from it. Remember, the key to improving is to develop solid PROCESS GOALS and not be so focused on OUTCOME GOALS. If you try all the shots in the drill and commit yourself to them, you will be learning—no matter where the ball goes. Part of what you develop in practice is trust, and trust comes from the experience of trying. Don't be afraid to fail. It is part of the learning process. **It's your world; claim it. It's your game; own it.** Hitting a shot left-handed (if you are right-handed) or hitting a shot with your eyes closed might seem like a silly thing to do, but it is all about developing trust and creativity.

Here are the rules for the 54-shot challenge:

- Warm up before you begin the drill. Approach the challenge as if it were a round of golf and prepare yourself in the same way you would prepare if you were going to go out and play. Be ready. Take this seriously.
- Do your full routine before every shot. Again, treat this as if it were a round of golf. Don't just "scrape-and-hit." Get into the THINK BOX. Cross the DECISION LINE and move into the PLAY BOX with full commitment to the shot you are hitting. If you get over the ball and you are thinking, "I can't hit this shot," back off, get into the THINK BOX again, and refocus your thoughts. A large part of what the 54-shot challenge is teaching you is to be committed to the task at hand no matter how difficult or unusual the task is. Some of these shots are deliberately designed to take you out of your comfort zone. They are designed to expand your comfort zone by teaching you to be more at ease and more focused in uncomfortable situations.
- Pick a target for every shot. Again, no scrape-and-hit here. The target must be specific—not just an area of the range—and your commitment to the target must be verbalized, at least internally if not out loud. Establish a relationship with the target. Make it the object of your

emotional energy. Want the target. Make everything flow toward it.

- Evaluate your shot on a scale of 1 to 5, with 5 being exactly what you intended to do. Remember, while you are judging OUTCOME here, your post-shot routine should be focused on PROCESS. Perhaps the shot warranted a 1 in terms of your intention for it, but you can still feel satisfied if you were fully committed to the shot.

Now let's begin with the 54-shot challenge.

- Hit five shots with five different clubs to five different targets. Pick any clubs you want, and the target can be any distance. Treat each shot as if it were a shot on the golf course. Take the club out of the bag, get into the THINK BOX, pick your target, verbalize your intentions, cross the DECISION LINE, and commit fully to the target in the PLAY BOX. Bring the same level of commitment and preparation to each of these five shots as you would bring if they were on the last hole of the last round of your life. Remember, the point here is not just to hit the shots but to be prepared to hit the shots. Score each of the five shots on the 1 to 5 scale. (Total: 5 shots.)
- Hit five shots each with the 8-iron, 6-iron, 4-iron, fairway wood, and driver. Change your target for each shot. The five shots with each club should include a high one, a low one, a left-to-right shot, a right-to-left shot, and a half shot. Don't say, "I can't hit the ball right to left." Try it!

Skills are developed by developing skills. New things are learned by trying new things. The important thing here is to TRY and to FOCUS on what you are trying to do. Remember, follow your pre-shot routine for each shot. Score each shot. (Total: 25 shots.)

- Turn a club around (maybe a 7-iron) and hit five lefty shots if you are right-handed or five righty shots if you are left-handed. This is about trust. This is about taking you out of your comfort zone. This is about making you realize that you can do things you have yet to even dream that you can do. This shot can also come in handy. A few times a year, you might find yourself up against a tree or a fence. This is also a great drill for balancing the body. Score each shot. (Total: 5 shots.)

- Hit a full 8-iron and notice the spot to which it carries. Now hit a 7-iron, 6-iron, 5-iron, fairway wood, and driver that carry to the same spot. This will help you develop a sense of feel for the clubs. It will help you find your hands, which are, after all, your only connection to the golf club. This is also a good drill for working on eye-hand coordination since you need to focus intently to hit shots with partial power. This will help you develop a sense of feel for the club and an awareness of different tempos. Score each shot. (Total: 6 shots.)

- Hit one 7-iron with your feet together. Hit one 7-iron standing on your left leg. Hit one 7-iron with your eyes closed. These three shots help with balance and trust—two absolute keys to good golf. Score each shot. (Total: 3 shots.)

- Hit five shots from divots with five different clubs. This is good for developing your shot-making, but it is also useful in teaching you not to rush into feeling victimized when you get a bad break on the golf course. Remember, giving yourself "princess lies" on the practice range does not prepare you for real golf. Again, follow your pre-shot routine for each shot. Score each shot. (Total: 5 shots.)
- Hit five shots with five different clubs to five different targets. This brings you back to where we started. Finish with the same focus and commitment with which you began the drill. Score each shot. (Total: 5 shots.)

Add up your score. While there is a perfect score for the 54-shot challenge (a 5 on each shot would be 270), your evaluation of your performance has to be focused on YOU. That is one of the great things about golf—our goals can be entirely personalized. Remember, VISION54 is a metaphor for what YOU want to achieve. We picked 18 consecutive birdies as the metaphor that reminds us that ANYTHING IS POSSIBLE. Once you have a score for yourself on the 54-shot challenge, then you have a measuring stick against which to rate yourself next time you try it. By trying to achieve your personal best on the practice range, you will become more successful at achieving your personal best on the golf course. By trying things outside your comfort zone, you will find that you are more comfortable when you have to hit an important shot under pressure.

54-SHOT CHALLENGE

ASSIGNMENT:

Do your full routine for every shot. Pick a target for every shot. Evaluate your shot on a scale of 1–5. Five is exactly what you intended to do.

You can choose different intentions to evaluate. Here are three suggestions:

1. Rate yourself if you execute the intended ball flight.
2. Rate yourself if you stayed committed to your PLAY BOX awareness or your specific PLAYING FOCUS.
3. You state your intention and a friend will evaluate or rate you.

1. Hit five shots with five different clubs, to five different targets.

2. Hit five shots with each club below changing the target between every shot. Hit a high, low, curving to the right, curving to the left, and a half shot with each club.

	8i	6i	4i	Fwy w	Driver
High	☐	☐	☐	☐	☐
Low	☐	☐	☐	☐	☐
Curving to the right	☐	☐	☐	☐	☐

Curving to the left ☐ ☐ ☐ ☐ ☐

A half shot ☐ ☐ ☐ ☐ ☐

3. Turn a club around (maybe a 7-iron) and hit five lefty shots if you play from the right, or righty shots if you play from the left.

☐ ☐ ☐ ☐ ☐

4. Hit a full 8-iron and look for the carry. Hit a 7i, 6i, 5i, Fwy w, and Driver that *carries* on the same spot.

☐ ☐ ☐ ☐ ☐ ☐

5. Hit one 7i with your feet together. Hit one 7i standing on your left leg. Hit one 7i with your eyes closed.

☐ ☐ ☐

6. Hit five shots from divots with five different clubs.

☐ ☐ ☐ ☐ ☐

7. Hit five shots with five different clubs to five different targets.

☐ ☐ ☐ ☐ ☐

Add up your score. My score today was: [＿＿＿＿＿＿]

54-SHOT CHALLENGE II

Here is another version of the 54-Shot Challenge. The same rules apply.

	9i	7i	5i	Fwy w	Driver
25% tempo	☐	☐	☐	☐	☐
50% tempo	☐	☐	☐	☐	☐
75% tempo	☐	☐	☐	☐	☐
100% tempo	☐	☐	☐	☐	☐

	6i	Fwy w
Extra high curving to the right	☐	☐
Extra low curving to the left	☐	☐
Extra low curving to the right	☐	☐
Extra high curving to the left	☐	☐
Punch or knockdown shot	☐	☐

Ten different shots with different clubs to different targets. Take 2–3 minutes' break between each shot.

☐ ☐ ☐ ☐ ☐ ☐ ☐ ☐ ☐ ☐

Swing using only your right arm, any club

☐

Swing using only your left arm, any club

☐

Swing standing only on your right foot, any club

☐

Swing standing only on your left foot, any club

☐

5 wedges, all with different ball flights that you call out before the swing

☐ ☐ ☐ ☐ ☐

5 drivers, all with different ball flights that you call out before the swing

☐ ☐ ☐ ☐ ☐

Add up your score.

☐

CHAPTER XX

The 30-Ball Practice Drill

"The thing always happens that you really believe in; and the belief in a thing makes it happen."

—FRANK LLOYD WRIGHT, ARCHITECT

SWING KEY: Practice golf; don't practice practice.

O ne reason it is difficult to take your practice range game out onto the golf course is because there is pressure on the golf course and no pressure on the range. As we have said throughout this book, practice is most valuable when it resembles real golf. Anyone can chip well when they chip five balls in a row to the same target from a perfect lie. Then they get out onto the golf course and draw a less-than-perfect lie to a difficult pin position and they wonder why they have no confidence in their ability to pull off the shot. Their practice did not get them ready for real golf, it got them ready for perfect golf. And that is not how the game is played.

A friend, who was a 2 handicap as a teenager before drifting away from the game for about twenty years as he developed a career and raised a family, and is now a 9 handicap, once said to us, "I'd rather be a 9 who once was a 2 than a 9 who once was a 15." What he meant was that his previous experience as a low single-digit handicap had taught him a variety of shots from a wide range of different conditions so that he was at least not surprised when faced with a challenging shot. He had experience with many different kinds of shots and thus was somewhat confident that he could pull them off. Any player can develop that sort of confidence through a well-planned practice routine. The 30-ball practice routine is such a routine.

Again, the mistake most people make when they practice is twofold: First, there is no focus to what they do. They merely swing the club and hit balls. Second, the way they are practicing has nothing to do with real golf. They are honing a sport that is not the game they play when they are on the golf course. **The key is to practice golf; don't practice practice.**

The purpose of the 30-ball practice routine, which was created by David Witt and Lynn when they worked with Chuck Hogan in the early 1990s, is to learn to be target focused. This not only helps you learn how to direct your full energy at the target, but it also teaches you how to hit shots under the pressure of performance since the outcome of the shots matters.

Here are the rules for this drill: Use only one ball at a time and focus on one task at a time. Don't stand there with a pile of balls in front of you. That tells your mind that the task is to make the pile of balls go away. The task is to learn to hit quality golf shots. Start with the short-game tasks first. The maximum number of balls to accomplish the full-shot task is 30—no exceptions. That means you can use up to 30 balls to accomplish the first task, and so on, through all ten tasks.

PUTTING

1. Make three six-footers. Two-putt three thirty-footers. Two-putt three sixty-footers. You can start out by performing each task three times, then you can make it more difficult by performing each task three CONSECUTIVE times. Remember, don't putt the SAME putt three times. Putt on three different lines. You must hit nine good putts from nine DIFFERENT positions.

CHIPPING

2. Hit three GOOD short chip shots. Hit three GOOD long chip shots. We will let you be the judge of what GOOD means here. It is defined entirely by where YOU are with YOUR game. We hope that the more you practice the more demanding you will be. Ideally, the goal will be that you chip to within one-putt distance. Eventually that can

be part of the drill—you move on only after you have chipped and made a one-putt. Again, vary the shot. Don't stand there with three balls at your feet, chipping to the same target.

PITCHING

3. Hit three GOOD short-pitch shots. Hit three GOOD long-pitch shots. Follow the same procedure as above. Make the shots challenging. And make them shots you have to THINK about. Remember, you are learning not just the shot but also the PROCESS of making the shot.

SAND

4. Hit three GOOD short sand shots. Hit three GOOD long sand shots. This is an area where OUTCOME goals need to take a backseat to PROCESS goals. Sand play is one of the areas where the recreational golfer most easily loses confidence. One of the most important benefits you can gain from this drill is bringing bunker play within your COMFORT ZONE. Make it a shot you are not afraid of.

FULL SHOTS

5. Hit one GOOD full sand wedge. Remember, a good shot is not only well struck but it is also target focused. Be happy with all aspects of the shot: your INTENTION, your ATTENTION to that intention, your COMMITMENT, your EXECUTION, and your POST-SHOT ROUTINE.

6. Hit one GOOD full pitching wedge. Eventually, GOOD will be something you FEEL, not something you judge.

7. Hit one GOOD full 9-iron. One of the values of this drill is that you will come to EXPECT to hit good shots. Progress is when the NORM moves to a different level. It is all about changing your beliefs and learning to expect more from yourself.

8. Hit one GOOD full shot, choosing one club from 8-iron through 4-iron. Perhaps, the first few times you do this drill, you pick the club with which you are the most comfortable. Later, pick the club you struggle with more. Remember, it is all about EXPANDING YOUR COMFORT ZONE.

9. Hit one GOOD full shot, choosing one club from 3-iron through 3-wood. Be REALLY SATISFIED with this shot. Set a high standard for yourself. Demand that EVERYTHING about the shot be GOOD.

10. Hit two GOOD drives. Again, start out with just needing two good drives, then raise the stakes to hitting two good drives consecutively. Full routine and full concentration. A GOOD drive involves not just where the ball went but where your mind was during the process. How ENGAGED were you when you hit the shot?

The purpose of these drills, as with all the practice plans we have devised, is not just to teach you a variety of shots but to ingrain in you a pre-shot and post-shot routine that will allow those shots to come out of you more often. This is FOCUSED PRACTICE. You are learning not just to swing the club but also about how to THINK while preparing to swing the club. The only way you can learn to be truly ENGAGED on the golf course is by being truly engaged when you are practicing. This drill simulates REAL GOLF PRESSURE and encourages you to develop the kind of concentration you need to succeed in real golf. This is not SCRAPE-AND-HIT. It is THINK-AND-HIT. In this routine, every shot truly has a purpose.

CHAPTER XXI

Good-Better-How?

"Some men see things as they are and say, 'Why?' I dream of things that never were and say, 'Why not?'"
—GEORGE BERNARD SHAW, PLAYWRIGHT

SWING KEY: It's about more than what you shot; it's about how you played.

So much of what we have talked about in this book is how the success of a golf shot is dependent on the preparation we bring to that shot. Have we built enough trust to bring full commitment to the shot? Can we execute the swing absent of any shred of a doubt about our ability to pull it off? The foundation for that trust is laid on the practice range and it is built upon in experience on the golf course. If there is one point we hope we have hammered home in this book, it is that the preparation to play great golf is a never-ending process. The preparation for the next round begins in the way we review the round we have just finished.

While conversations about score or who won the bet are appropriate talk in the grillroom after a round, your internal discussion of your day on the golf course should be very different. It should not be OUTCOME-oriented but rather focused on the PROCESS, your COMMITMENT to it, and what you learned from the round that can benefit your play in the future. There are three essential questions to ask yourself after a round of golf:

1. What was GOOD about my game today?
2. What could I do BETTER?
3. HOW can I improve those aspects of my game where I need to do better?

GOOD? BETTER? HOW? Notice that all of the questions are positively framed. We never ask what we did wrong. Give yourself this quiz after a round:

1. What did I learn today?
2. What experience do I want to remember from today's round?
3. What was the one critical decision I made today?
4. If I could have done one thing differently in my round today, what would that be?

How we think about a round after we have played it is as important as how we have prepared for the round. There is good in every experience, no matter what the outcome. There is learning in all we do. The round you have just finished is the beginning of the preparation for the next round. Remember, you are creating an emotional memory on which your mind and body will draw in the future. Consider this "golf therapy." You will find that your true self is most exposed under pressure—both on the golf course and off. It is all about self-understanding, learning to manage what you want to remember, and always making sure your honest evaluation of yourself ends up being translated into action! **It's about more than what you shot, it's about how you played.**

Here is a sample evaluation from one of the players we coach:

GOOD:

1. Course management. This was very important because of the way the course was set up.
2. I hit great tee shots all week on a tight course.
3. I hit a lot of great iron shots.
4. I hit a lot of good putts.
5. I did a good job of playing with my clubs and knowing that they did not fit me properly.
6. I walked on Tuesday and Wednesday, which was a great way for me to maintain a good pace of play for myself. It also limited the amount of time I had to wait on the group in front of me.
7. I chose some great games within the game. I came up with one to reward myself for hitting good putts within two feet of the hole, even if I didn't make them.

8. I did a great job of leaving my round at the golf course and not letting my performance alter my feelings of self-worth.

9. I hit a great shot around a tree and onto a green.

10. I two-putted the hardest green on the course.

BETTER:

1. I could have been more patient and done a better job of minimizing the level of frustration I allowed myself to feel and dealt with that frustration in a way that did not snowball. I could have been less judgmental about shots that I did not execute the way I wanted to.

2. I could have focused less on scoring and outcome.

3. I could have hit better wedge shots.

HOW:

1. I need to find a way to balance segments of my personality better. I started out by swinging freely, one shot at a time. When I didn't score the way I wanted to, I tried to find a different way to score and abandoned my game plan.

2. I need to make sure that my goals and expectations, and the expectations of others, do not conflict with or work against my PLAYING FOCUS. My PLAYING FOCUS needs to be my sole focus. Score needs to be a distant second.

3. I need to be in this mind-set before, during, and after every round.

4. I need to make sure that my routine and what I do during each round minimizes the amount of time that I need to

be focused, so that I can be completely focused for each shot. I think I need to look at different things that I can do when I am not focused.

5. I need to get equipment that fits me so that my wedges and irons don't have very different lies.

6. I need to practice my wedges so that my distance control is more precise. I can do this by practicing different shots to different distances.

7. I can practice making putts within twenty feet under pressure.

8. I can simulate situations where I have to overcome frustration and poor results, and try to improve execution and scoring. I need to simulate making bogeys and then simulate trying to make birdies to improve my score.

9. More than anything else, this experience reminds me how important it is for me to avoid getting too caught up in expectations and results. This can be difficult when you feel that you should be able to perform well.

Why is it important to review a round in this way? Well, there is an expression that says, "What you put your attention on has a tendency to grow." What does that mean? It means that what you focus on gets stored in your brain, and if there is emotion attached to the experience, it gets stored even more strongly. Emotions are like a highlighter to the brain. If you want to remember something, good or bad, highlight it with a charged emotion. The research on emotional intelligence shows that a person will often avoid learning environments and challenges that give rise to unpleasant feelings that have been embedded in neural tracks in the brain from an earlier time.

If you want to build a solid base of self-esteem and confidence, then focus on what is working well. There really is a science to "go to your happy place" and positive self-talk. The memories you have stored in the brain are the ones that will show up when you are faced with a similar situation in the future. When you stand on the first tee, face a difficult bunker shot, or play in an important match, what signals do you want your senses to send you? It all depends on what you have emotionalized in the past.

After a practice or performance, you might want to ask, "How did it go?" or, "How are you doing?" The first feedback or evaluation question could be, "What was GOOD and what was FUN?"

Since one of the intentions of feedback and evaluation is to receive information and keep on improving, the next question could be, "What can be BETTER?"

Through our experiences as coaches, we have found a lot more positive response from players when we use the "better" word instead of what is wrong, bad, or weak. It seems to create more energy and drive forward. Development is about making changes that lead to improvements. Be aware of how many "betters" you can handle. Too many changes often lead to confusion and unproductive stress. If you are not sure, start with ONE!

The last question may be the most important of them all: "HOW are you going to do it?" It's fine to spend time evaluating what is working well and what can be done better.

But then it comes time to put that talk into action. That is what the HOW question will help with. Where, when, how often, and other specific questions that lead to a concrete action plan can also be asked at this time.

- What is GOOD?
- What can be BETTER?
- HOW are you going to do it?

These three questions create an environment and INTENTION to help you build confidence and self-esteem. One of our goals is for you to learn how to become your own best coach. One simple but profound strategy that we have found that works toward this end is to be consistent in asking the GOOD, BETTER, HOW questions and listening to your answers. It is a self-imposed pop quiz and forces you to understand your game better and be more honest with yourself. We find that posing the questions leads to positive actions. **Quiz yourself, listen to yourself, and grow. The first step toward playing better in the future is having a better understanding of how you are playing now.**

CHAPTER XXII

VISION54: Make It the Way You See the Game

"The purpose of life is a life of purpose."

—ROBERT BYRNE, HUMORIST

SWING KEY: Every shot must have a purpose.

Golf is an amazing game. There is perhaps no other activity that brings us into such close contact with ourselves. Unlike in other sports, the pace at which golf unfolds makes it impossible for us to run away from our minds. Unlike other intellectual activities, we have to integrate our physical selves into any equation for success. To reach our potential, we must learn how to function successfully as human beings. It is about trust and understanding and commitment. It is about having a purpose—having a meaning—and then pursuing it.

One of the reasons golf is so compelling is that the fears and doubts we face on a golf course are likely not all that dissimilar from the fears and doubts we confront in our everyday lives. In fact, one of the things that makes golf such a challenge to master is that, in the end, it is all about us. Unlike in other sports, there is no place to hide on a golf course. It comes down to this: You have to swing the club and you are bringing a lifetime of successes and failures to that shot.

One of the things we hope you have learned from this book is that your past does not have to be your future. Just because you do not have a track record of playing your best when it matters the most does not mean that that always has to be the case. Your golf reality has a history, but it also has a future, and the nature of that future is entirely in your control. You can change your reality by changing your beliefs. **VISION54 is a metaphor for your dreams, and you can make your dreams happen by believing that they can happen.**

Of course, belief alone gets you nowhere. It needs to be combined with action. One of the other things we hope you have learned from this book is that success is the product of commitment. A good golf shot occurs in a blur, a mere matter of seconds, but the preparation for that shot was much more extensive. Your time in the THINK BOX will always be greater than your time in the PLAY BOX.

The shot you are about to hit right now started on the practice range where you were simulating real golf. It had its roots in the last round you played when you concluded the day's activities by asking the Good–Better–How? questions. It is being

performed against the backdrop of the emotional memory created from the post-shot reaction to the previous shot—or a
previous shot like this one months ago. It is being carried out
only after you have done your job in the THINK BOX and
crossed the DECISION LINE into the PLAY BOX. This shot
you are hitting right now is about every shot you have ever hit.

To reach your potential as a player, you need to explore
your potential as a person, and we all possess much more potential than we ever tap into. That is an exciting realization to
make. No matter who we are, no matter what our skill level,
we are not playing golf up to our full potential. We can all get
better. There is absolutely no reason why that is not true.
There is more good golf within us. We just have to find it and
let it out. Once we are aware that it is there, once we admit that
our potential is greater than our performance, we have rocked
the world of our beliefs and made anything and everything
possible. It's all about becoming aware of what is possible.

The dictionary says that the word "aware" implies knowledge gained through one's own perceptions or by means of information. Synonyms for awareness include: alertness, aliveness,
appreciation, apprehension, attention, attentiveness, conscious-
ness, enlightenment, experience, familiarity, information, keen-
ness, mindfulness, perception, realization, recognition, sensibility,
and understanding.

To most thoroughly explore our potential, we must become aware of several aspects of the way we are:

• The expenditure of physical and mental effort in work is as
  natural as play and rest.

- People will exercise self-direction and control toward achieving objectives they are committed to.
- People want to achieve.
- People learn to accept and seek responsibility.
- People have the capacity to exercise a high degree of imagination, ingenuity, and creativity.

This is where awareness comes in. All learning begins with awareness. All growth is first about awareness of oneself (physically, mentally, and emotionally), the golf club, the golf ball, the course, and the game.

Awareness really begins with honesty. Honesty is required if we want to attain balance and peak performance. This is one of Annika Sorenstam's great assets. She is more honest and aware than just about any other player we have been around. She is aware of her body, thoughts, and emotions. She catches herself sooner than most players when something is different from what it needs to be for peak performance. On top of that, Annika has found her own unique tools to manage herself from that awareness. From that position, she can create her own best game.

We know that every day in life and on the golf course is going to be different. This change is internal as well as external. Things are always changing in our bodies, minds, and emotions. The conditions around us are constantly changing . . . the weather, the golf course, and other people. The only constant is change. Often, we hear from students that they would like to be more consistent. If you really want to develop consistency you must begin by being fully aware. Know what is going on around you and adjust to it.

If you are honest about where you are at the moment and take responsibility for making the changes that are required, then it's possible to make the necessary choices to be as good as you can be from day to day. You are the one holding the golf club, affecting the contact with the ball, and experiencing your thoughts and emotions. With increased awareness, you will be better equipped to coach yourself in all of the elements of the game. To be aware, we need to be in the present moment.

If a player isn't aware of what he or she is doing, it doesn't matter how much the teacher knows. Have you ever stopped to consider how much time in your day you're fully present?

There's an old Zen teaching story that speaks to this. The master is asked by the student:

"How do you put enlightenment into action? How do you practice it in everyday life?"

"I put enlightenment into action," replies the master, "by eating and sleeping."

"But everyone sleeps and everyone eats," replies the student.

"Quite so," says the master, "but it is a very rare person who really eats when they eat and really sleeps when they sleep."

Real learning and change can take place only when we commit to being present with full awareness. The cultivation of awareness and balance is a lifelong process. If you practice awareness, you will be surprised at your ability to change, radically and dramatically. So many of the problems we experience on the golf course stem from the fact that we fear failure or that we remember a time when we had the same shot and botched it. Our past does not have to be our future if we merely change our beliefs and accept that we can create a new golfing reality. **The first step is to realize that every shot must have a purpose.**

In *Alice in Wonderland,* when Alice takes the pill that makes her large, she asks the knob on the locked door how she can get to the other side. The doorknob tells Alice to crawl through the keyhole, to which Alice replies: "I can't, it's impossible." And the doorknob answers: "No, it's impassible. Nothing's impossible." Exactly, my friend, exactly.

Recommended Reading

Golf Annika's Way by Annika Sorenstam (Gotham Books, 2004).

Golf Parent for the Future by Lynn Marriott and Pia Nilsson (VISION54/Coaching for the Future, Inc., 2003).

The HeartMath Solution: The HeartMath Institute's Revolutionary Program for Engaging the Power of the Heart's Intelligence by Doc Childre and Howard Martin (HarperSanFrancisco, 1999).

Mastery: The Keys to Success and Long-Term Fullfillment by George Leonard (Plume, 1992).

Quantum Golf: The Path to Golf Mastery by Kjell Enhager and Samantha Wallace (Warner Books, 1992).

Rethinking Golf: A New Approach to Performance in the 21st Century by Chuck Hogan (Maverick Publications, 2001).

Sport Parent for the Future by Lynn Marriott and Pia Nilsson (VISION54/Coaching for the Future, Inc., 2005).

What Happy People Know: How the New Science of Happiness Can Change Your Life for the Better by Dan Baker and Cameron Stauth (Rodale Books, 2003).

GOLF54® Programs

If you are interested in getting the ball in the hole in fewer strokes and are committed to learning and experiencing the game with an integrated approach, we welcome you to attend a GOLF54 program.

For more information and to register for a GOLF54 program, go to *www.golf54.com*.